THE CONTEMPORARY SHAKESPEARE

Edited by A.L. Rowse

The Tempest

Modern Text with Introduction

UNIVERSITY PRESS OF AMERICA

University Press of America,™ Inc.

4720 Boston Way
Lanham, MD 20706

3 Henrietta Street
London WC2E 8LU England

Distributed to the trade by The Scribner Book Companies

Library of Congress Cataloging in Publication Data

Shakespeare, William, 1564-1616.
  The Tempest.

  (The Contemporary Shakespeare)
  I. Rowse, A.L. (Alfred Leslie), 1903-
II. Title. III. Series: Shakespeare, William, 1564-1616.
Plays (University Press of America : Pbk. ed.)
PR2833.A2R66   1984   822.3'3   84-5070
ISBN 0-8191-3899-1 (pbk.)

This play is also available as part of Volume I in a six volume clothbound
and slipcased set.

Book design by Leon Bolognese

WHY A CONTEMPORARY SHAKESPEARE?

The starting point of my project was when I learned both from television and in education, that Shakespeare is being increasingly dropped in schools and colleges because of the difficulty of the language. In some cases, I gather, they are given just a synopsis of the play, then the teacher or professor embroiders from his notes.

This is deplorable. We do not want Shakespeare progressively dropped because of superfluous difficulties that can be removed, skilfully, conservatively, keeping to every line of the text. Nor must we look at the question statically, for this state of affairs will worsen as time goes on and we get further away from the language of 400 years ago—difficult enough in all conscience now.

We must begin by ridding our mind of prejudice, i.e. we must not pre-judge the matter. A friend of mine on New York radio said that he was 'appalled' at the very idea; but when he heard my exposition of what was proposed he found it reasonable and convincing.

Just remember, I do not need it myself: *I live in the Elizabethan age*, Shakespeare's time, and have done for years, and am familiar with its language, and his. But even for me there are still difficulties—still more for modern people, whom I am out to help.

Who, precisely?

Not only students at school and in college, but all readers of Shakespeare. Not only those, but all viewers of the plays, in the theatre, on radio and television—actors too, who increasingly find pronunciation of the words difficult, particularly obsolete ones—and there are many, besides the difficulty of accentuation.

The difficulties are naturally far greater for non-English-speaking peoples. We must remember that he is our greatest asset, and that other peoples use him a great deal in learning our language. There are no Iron Curtains for him—though, during Mao's Cultural Revolution in China, he was prohibited. Now that the ban has been lifted, I learn that the Chinese in thousands flock to his plays.

Now, a good deal that was grammatical four hundred years ago is positively ungrammatical today. We might begin by removing what is no longer good grammar.

For example: plural subjects with a verb in the singular:

'*Is* Bushy, Green and the earl of Wiltshire dead?' Any objection to replacing 'is' correctly by 'are'? Certainly not. I notice that some modern editions already correct—

These high wild hills and rough uneven ways

Draw*s* out our miles and make*s* them wearisome

to 'draw' and 'make', quite sensibly. Then, why not go further and regularise this Elizabethan usage to modern, consistently throughout?

Similarly with archaic double negatives—'Nor shall you not think neither'—and double comparatives: 'this is more worser than before.' There are hundreds of instances of what is now just bad grammar to begin with.

There must be a few thousand instances of superfluous subjunctives to reduce to simplicity and sense. Today we use the subjunctive occasionally after 'if', when we say 'if it be'. But we mostly say today 'if it is'. Now Shakespeare has hundreds of subjunctives, not only after if, but after though, although, unless, lest, whether, until, till, etc.

I see no point whatever in retaining them. They only add superfluous trouble in learning English, when the great appeal of our language as a world-language is precisely that it has less grammar to learn than almost any. Russian is unbelievably complicated. Inflected languages—German is like Latin in this respect—are really rather backward; it has been a great recommendation that English has been more progressive in this respect in simplifying itself.

Now we can go further along this line: keep a few subjunctives, if you must, but reduce them to a minimum.

Let us come to the verb. It is a great recommendation to modern English that our verbs are comparatively simple to conjugate—unlike even French, for example. In the Elizabethan age there was a great deal more of it, and some of it inconsistent in modern usage. Take Shakespeare's,

'Where is thy husband now? Where be thy brothers?'

Nothing is lost by rendering this as we should today:

Where is your husband now? Where are your brothers?

And so on.

The second and third person singular—all those shouldsts and wouldsts, wilts and sh─── ─ ─

simplification may be effected—with no loss as far as I
can see, and with advantages from several points of view.

For example, 'st' at the end of a word is rather difficult to say, and more difficult even for us when it is
succeeded by a word beginning with 'th'. Try saying,
'Why usurpedst thou this?' Foreigners have the greatest
difficulty in pronouncing our 'th' anyway—many never
succeed in getting it round their tongues. Many of these
tongue-twisters even for us proliferate in Shakespeare,
and I see no objection to getting rid of *superfluous* difficulties. Much easier for people to say, 'Why did you
usurp this?'—the same number of syllables too.

This pre-supposes getting rid of almost all thous and
thees and thines. I have no objection to keeping a few
here and there, if needed for a rhyme—even then they
are sometimes not necessary.

Some words in Shakespeare have changed their
meaning into the exact opposite: we ought to remove
that stumbling-block. When Hamlet says, 'By heaven,
I'll make a ghost of him that *lets* me', he means *stops*;
and we should replace it by stops, or holds me.
Shakespeare regularly uses the word 'owe' where we
should say own: the meaning has changed. Take a line
like, 'Thou dost here usurp the name thou ow'st not':
we should say, 'You do here usurp the name you own
not', with the bonus of getting rid of two ugly 'sts'.

The word 'presently' in the Elizabethan age did not
mean in a few minutes or so, but immediately—in-
stantly has the same number of syllables. 'Prevent'
then had its Latin meaning, to go before, or forestall.
Shakespeare frequently uses the word 'still' for always
or ever.

Let us take the case of many archaic forms of words,
simple one-syllable words that can be replaced without
the slightest difference to the scansion: 'sith' for since,

'wrack' for wreck, 'holp' for helped, 'writ' for wrote, 'brake' for broke, 'spake' for spoke, 'bare' for bore, etc.

These give no trouble, nor do a lot of other words that he uses: 'repeal' for recall, 'reproof' for disproof, 'decline' for incline. A few words do give more trouble. The linguistic scholar, C. T. Onions, notes that it is sometimes difficult to give the precise meaning Shakespeare attaches to the word 'conceit'; it usually means thought, or fancy, or concept. I do not know that it ever has our meaning; actually the word 'conceited' with him means ingenious or fantastic, as 'artificial' with Elizabethans meant artistic or ingenious.

There is a whole class of words that have completely gone out, of which moderns do not know the meaning. I find no harm in replacing the word 'coistrel' by rascal, which is what it means—actually it has much the same sound—or 'coil' by fuss; we find 'accite' for summon, 'indigest' for formless. Hamlet's word 'reechy', for the incestuous kisses of his mother and her brother-in-law, has gone out of use: the nearest word, I suppose, would be reeky, but filthy would be a suitable modern equivalent.

In many cases it is extraordinary how little one would need to change, how conservative one could be. Take Hamlet's famous soliloquy, 'To be or not to be.' I find only two words that moderns would not know the meaning of, and one of those we might guess:

> . . .When he himself might his *quietus* make
>   With a bare bodkin? Who would *fardels* bear. . .

'Quietus' means put paid; Elizabethans wrote the Latin 'quietus est' at the bottom of a bill that was paid—when it was—to say that it was settled. So that you could replace 'quietus' by settlement, same number of syllables, though not the same accentuation; so I would prefer to use the word acquittance, which has both.

'Fardels' means burdens; I see no objection to rendering, 'Who would burdens bear'—same meaning, same number of syllables, same accent: quite simple. I expect all the ladies to know what a bodkin is: a long pin, or skewer.

Now let us take something really difficult—perhaps the most difficult passage to render in all Shakespeare. It is the virtuoso comic piece describing all the diseases that horseflesh is heir to, in *The Taming of the Shrew*. The horse is Petruchio's. President Reagan tells me that this is the one Shakespearean part that he played—and a very gallant one too. In Britain last year we saw a fine performance of his on horseback in Windsor Park along-side of Queen Elizabeth II—very familiar ground to William Shakespeare and Queen Elizabeth I, as we know from *The Merry Wives of Windsor*.

Here is a headache for us: Petruchio's horse (not President Reagan's steed) was 'possessed with the glanders, and like to mose in the chine; troubled with the lampass, infected with the fashions, full of windgalls, sped with spavins, rayed with the yellows, past cure of the fives, stark spoiled with the staggers, begnawn with the bots; swayed in the back, and shoulder-shotten; near-legged before, and with a half-cheeked bit, and a headstall of sheep's leather', etc.

What on earth are we to make of that? No doubt it raised a laugh with Elizabethans, much more familiarly acquainted with horseflesh than we are; but I doubt if Hollywood was able to produce a nag for Reagan that qualified in all these respects.

Now, even without his horsemanship, we can clear one fence at the outset: 'mose in the chine'. Pages of superfluous commentary have been devoted to that word 'mose'. There was no such Elizabethan word: it was simply a printer's misprint for 'mourn', meaning dripping or running; so it suggests a running sore. You would need to consult the *Oxford English Dictionary*, compiled on historical lines, for some of the words, others like 'glanders' country folk know and we can guess.

So I would suggest a rendering something like this: 'possessed with glanders, and with a running sore in the back; troubled in the gums, and infected in the glands; full of galls in the fetlocks and swollen in the joints; yellow with jaundice, past cure of the strangles; stark spoiled with the staggers, and gnawed by worms; swayed in the back and shoulder put out; near-legged before, and with a half-cheeked bit and headgear of sheep's leather', etc. That at least makes it intelligible.

Oddly enough, one encounters the greatest difficulty with the least important words and phrases, Elizabethan expletives and malapropisms, or salutations like God 'ild you, Godden, for God shield you, Good-even, and so on. 'God's wounds' was Elizabeth I's favourite swearword; it appears frequently enough in Victorian novels as 'Zounds'— I have never heard anyone use it. The word 'Marry!', as in the phrase 'Marry come up!' has similarly gone out, though a very old gentleman at All Souls, Sir Charles Oman, had heard the phrase in the back-streets of Oxford just after the 1914-18 war. 'Whoreson' is frequent on the lips of coarse fellows in Shakespeare: the equivalent in Britain today would be bloody, in America (I suppose) s.o.b.

Relative pronouns, who and which: today we use who for persons, which for things. In Elizabethan times the two were hardly distinguished and were interchangeable. Provokingly Shakespeare used the personal relative 'who' more frequently for impersonal objects, rivers, buildings, towns; and then he no less frequently uses 'which' for persons. This calls out to be regularised for the modern reader.

Other usages are more confusing. The word 'cousin'

was used far more widely by the Elizabethans for their kin: it included nephews, for instance. Thus it is confusing in the English History plays to find a whole lot of nephews—like Richard III's, whom he had made away with in the Tower of London—referred to and addressed as cousins. That needs regularisation today, in the interests of historical accuracy and to get the relationship clear. The word 'niece' was sometimes used of a grand-child—in fact this is the word Shakespeare used in his will for his little grand-daughter Elizabeth, his eventual heiress who ended up as Lady Barnard, leaving money to her poor relations the Hathaways at Stratford. The Latin word *neptis*, from which niece comes also meant grand-child—Shakespeare's grammar-school education at Stratford was in Latin, and this shows you that he often thought of a word in terms of its Latin derivation.

Malapropisms, misuse of words, sometimes mistaking of meanings, are frequent with uneducated people, and sometimes not only with those. Shakespeare transcribed them from lower-class life to raise a laugh, more frequently than any writer for the purpose. They are an endearing feature of the talk of Mistress Quickly, hostess of the Boar's Inn in East Cheapside, and we have no difficulty in making out what she means. But in case some of us do, and for the benefit of non-native English speakers, I propose the correct word in brackets afterwards: 'You have brought her into such a canaries [quandary]. . .and she's as fartuous [virtuous] a civil, modest wife. . .'

Abbreviations: Shakespeare's text is starred—and in my view, marred—by innumerable abbreviations, which not only look ugly on the page but are sometimes difficult to pronounce. It is not easy to pronounce 'is't', or 'in't', or 'on't', and some others: if we cannot get rid of them altogether they should be drastically reduced. Similarly with 'i'th'', 'o'th'', with which the later plays are liberally bespattered, for in the or of the.

We also have a quite unnecessary spattering of apostrophes in practically all editions of the plays—''d' for the past participle, e.g. 'gather'd'. Surely it is much better to regularise the past participle 'ed', e.g. gathered; and when the last syllable is, far less frequently, to be pronounced, then accent it, gatheréd.

This leads into the technical question of scansion, where a practising poet is necessary to get the accents right, to help the reader, and still more the actor. Most people will hardly notice that, very often, the frequent ending of words in 'ion', like reputation, has to be pronounced with two syllables at the end. So I propose to accent this when necessary, e.g. reputatiòn. I have noticed the word 'ocean' as tri-syllabic, so I accent it, to help, oceàn. A number of words which to us are monosyllables were pronounced as two: hour, fire, tired; I sometimes accent or give them a dieresis, either hoùr or fïre. In New England speech words like prayèr, thëre, are apt to be pronounced as two syllables—closer to Elizabethan usage (as with words like gotten) than is modern speech in Britain.

What I notice in practically all editions of Shakespeare's plays is that the editors cannot be relied on to put the accents in the right places. One play edited by a well known Shakespearean editor had, I observed, a dozen accents placed over the wrong syllables. This is understandable, for these people don't write poetry and do not know how to scan. William Shakespeare knew all about scanning, and you need to be both familiar with Elizabethan usage and a practising traditional poet to be able to follow him.

His earlier verse was fairly regular in scansion, mostly iambic pentameter with a great deal of rhyme. As time went on he loosened out, until there are numerous irregular lines—this leaves us much freer in the matter of modernising. Our equivalents should be rhythmically as close as possible, but a strait-jacket need be no part of the equipment. A good Shakespearean scholar tells us, 'there is no necessity for Shakespeare's lines to scan absolutely. He thought of his verse as spoken rather than written and of his rhythmic units in terms of the voice rather than the page.'

There is nothing exclusive or mandatory about my project. We can all read Shakespeare in any edition we like—in the rebarbative olde Englishe spelling of the First Folio, if we wish. Any number of conventional academic editions exist, all weighed down with a burden of notes, many of them superfluous. I propose to make most of them unnecessary—only one occasionally at the foot of very few pages. Let the text be freed of superfluous difficulties, remove obstacles to let it speak for itself, while adhering conservatively to every line.

We really do not need any more editions of the Plays on conventional lines—more than enough of those exist already. But *A Contemporary Shakespeare* on these lines—both revolutionary and conservative—should be a help to everybody all round the world—though especially for younger people, increasingly with time moving away from the language of 400 years ago.

INTRODUCTION

he *Tempest*, of 1611, is Shakespeare's penulti-
mate play, with the atmosphere of farewell in it,
as in *Henry VIII*, last of all. Yet it was placed first
when the First Folio was published in 1623, and still
appears first, absurdly, in most editions of the Works.
This is apt to put people wrong, especially in previous
centuries, when they were uncertain of the chronology
of the Plays. How could one hope to estimate Beethoven's
work aright, if one thought that the last Quartets came
first? In the 18th century, as Dr. Johnson tells us,
people did 'know not the exact date of this or the other
plays', and therefore 'cannot tell how our author might
have changed his practice or opinions.' More than this,
it is impossible to appreciate the development of
Shakespeare's mind, the expansion of his art, or the
manner and circumstances of its flowering in response
to both his own experience and his experience of his
time, without a reliable chronology of his work. This is
where an Elizabethan historian comes in, is indeed
indispensable.

The Tempest was performed before James I at
Whitehall, on Hallowmas night, 1 November 1611.
Only two years before, in 1609 the Second Charter of
the Virginia Company had been issued—a national
venture to which hundreds of people subscribed, from

13

the Archbishop of Canterbury and the Earls of Southampton and Pembroke downwards, to give a solid foundation to the first English colony in America, based upon Jamestown. And Shakespeare had a number of acquaintances in the Virginia Company. But that year the flagship of the fleet going out there, the *Sea Venture*, met with a tornado off Bermuda—'the still-vexed Bermoothes'—ran in on the rocks a wreck, and yet not a life lost.

We shall see all through this modern, yet historically minded, edition how closely Shakespeare responded to the challenge of topical circumstances, from Normandy in 1591, onwards. His box-office sense would indicate that anyway. Now, in the last years of his career, with the war ended and the door to settlement in North America open—for which partly it had been fought—the country was full of interest in the overseas voyages. In consequence Shakespeare's last plays, from *Pericles* (1608) onwards, are full of sea-voyages, wrecks, partings and renewals.

An account of the island wreck was published in 1610: Jourdan's *A Discovery of the Bermudas, otherwise called the Isle of Devils*. But Shakespeare had a closer source of information in the manuscript letter sent back to Blackfriars by William Strachey, Secretary to Virginia. Strachey was closely associated with Black-friars—as Shakespeare had been from the early days when his Stratford fellow, Richard Field, printed his long poems there, and now from 1608 more than ever as part-owner of the theatre within. The play follows Strachey's account of the tornado, down to the St. Elmo's fire-ball running down the rigging, the break-up of the ship, and yet no one lost.

To contemporaries the uninhabited island was enchanted, vexed not only by storms but by spirits. And

the dominant theme of the play is magic, that of
Prospero and Ariel, their charms and incantations,
while Caliban the only indigenous inhabitant had had a
witch for a mother. Here was another strong appeal for
contemporaries, with 'Dr.' Forman now much to the
fore, and Dr. Dee familiar in the background.

Caliban is the most original creation in the play,
entirely of Shakespeare's making, the obvious product
of his reading and reflecting on the voyages,
notably—but not only—Hakluyt. He looked into
Eden's History of Travel, whence he got the name
Setebos; and he made use of friend Florio's translation
of Montaigne's essay on cannibals for a very different
exposure of primitive communism. Dr. Johnson saw,
rightly, that he was a 'diligent reader.'

Caliban's speeches clearly reflect Hariot's descrip-
tions in his *Brief and True Report of the New-found-
land of Virginia*. Recognisably in—

>   When you came first
> You stroke me and made much of me; would give me
> Water with berries in it; and teach me how
> To name the bigger light, and how the less
> That burn by day and night.

Hariot had astonished the Indians by showing them the
sun and moon through his rudimentary telescope.

>   And then I loved you,
> And showed you all the qualities of the isle,
>   The fresh springs, brine pits, barren place and fertile.

This is as it had been on Roanoke in 1585–6. But it is
the rascally Stephano and Trinculo, realistic enough as
they are, not Prospero the exiled Duke with his magic
power, who get the poor savage drunk—a portent in its
way of what was to happen to the Indians from fire-
water in the progress of colonisation.

Progress? We see that William Shakespeare had no illusions about primitive man, the state of nature, and all the nonsense about primeval innocence and communism. He puts these ideas into the mouth of a councillor, as it might be of the Leftist Greater London Council today:

In the commonwealth I would by contraries
Execute all things; for no kind of traffic
Would I admit; no name of magistrate;
Letters should not be known—

we remember Jack Cade's hatred of letters and book-learning, from the earliest play—

riches and poverty,
And use of service, none; contract, succession,
Bourn, bound of land, tilth, vineyard, none;
No use of metal, corn, or wine, or oil;
No occupation; all men idle, all.

The women were all to be innocent and pure—no disease: very unlike contemporary life.

All things in common Nature should produce
Without sweat or endeavour: treason, felony,
Sword, pike, knife, gun, or need of any engine,
Would I not have . . .

To this a questioner asks:
No marrying among his subjects?

The reply is no doubt William Shakespeare's:

None, man, all idle: whores and knaves.

This is much like what happened in early days in Virginia, according to Captain John Smith: instead of planting, the colonists played bowls or dug for gold—then starved. And Shakespeare took the reports of gold-digging up into *Timon of Athens*.[1]

---

[1] cf my *The Elizabethans and America*, 192.

Magic was much in the air at this time, with a king too on the throne who was an expert in demonology—and this must have been something new for the audience at Blackfriars, always on the alert for anything new. Caliban thinks Prospero's power is in his books:

> First, to possess his books: for without them
> He's but a sot, as I am, and has not
> One spirit in his command . . .
> Burn but his books.

Prospero is properly mysterious, as a kind of *magus*. Nor is it unlikely that that other magus had himself in mind in his farewell to his art:

> I'll break my staff,
> Bury it certain fathoms in the earth,
> And deeper than did ever plummet sound
> I'll drown my book.

It certainly sounds a personal note of renunciation. *Henry VIII* may have been called for some special occasion—otherwise there is a remarkable, if understandable, silence from the gentleman of Stratford.

One would think that the play was written in the country, not only from the more elaborate stage directions, as if for someone else to produce in London. But also from the marvellous evocations of countryside:

> You elves of hills, brooks, standing lakes, and
>   groves . . .
>   You demi-puppets that
> By moonshine do the green, sour ringlets make,
> Whereof the ewe not bites; and you whose pastime
> Is to make midnight mushrooms, that rejoice
> To hear the solemn curfew . . .

How much this countryman loved the English countryside, and with what close observation! Here, for example, we have the image 'as fast as mill-wheels strike', or tears running down 'like winter's drops from eaves of reeds', i.e. rush-roofed cottages.

How unlike Marlowe! And yet Marlowe is present in mind at the end, as at the beginning. In the magical song, 'Come unto these yellow sands', the phrase 'the wild waves whist' is Marlowe's—after all those years, and all that had happened in between. The phrase 'full fathom five' goes back to *Romeo and Juliet*. It is as if Shakespeare, with infallible sense of propriety, were rounding things up. So too with the Epilogue:

> Now my charms are all o'erthrown,
> And what strength I have's my own.

Then, in the way he had all along sought favour with the audience, unlike Ben Jonson:

> Gentle breath of yours my sails
> Must fill, or else my project fails—
> Which was to please.

Ben was not pleased. He said of his own work, 'if there is never a servant monster [i.e. Caliban] in the fair, who can help it? Nor a nest of antics [buffoons]. He is loth to make Nature afraid in his plays, like those that beget *Tales* [i.e. Winter's Tales], *Tempests*, and such-like drolleries.' The drolleries were more popular than his works and moreover, more enduring. The intellectuals of the time, wrong as usual, thought more highly of Ben Jonson. Shakespeare, even at the end of his career, certainly found something new—as had been his wont all along—in this fairy tale of the enchanted island.

CHARACTERS

ALONSO, King of Naples
SEBASTIAN, his brother
PROSPERO, the rightful Duke of Milan
ANTONIO, his brother, the usurping Duke of Milan
FERDINAND, son of the King of Naples
GONZALO, an honest old councillor
ADRIAN ⎫
FRANCISCO ⎭ lords
CALIBAN, a primitive slave
TRINCULO, a jester
STEPHANO, a butler
Master of a ship, Boatswain, Mariners
MIRANDA, daughter of Prospero
ARIEL, a spirit
IRIS, CERES, JUNO, Nymphs, and Reapers, characters
in the masque, played by Ariel and Spirits

Act I

SCENE I
A ship at sea.

*Thunder and lightning. Enter a Shipmaster
and a Boatswain.*

MASTER Boatswain!

BOATSWAIN Here, Master. What cheer?

MASTER Good. Speak to the mariners. Fall to it, sharp,
or we run ourselves aground. Bestir, bestir! *Exit*

Enter Mariners

BOATSWAIN Heigh, my hearts! Cheerily, cheerily,
my hearts! Quick, quick! Take in the topsail!
Attend to the Master's whistle!—Blow till you
burst your wind, if room enough.

Enter ALONSO, SEBASTIAN, ANTONIO, FERDINAND,
GONZALO, *and others.*

ALONSO Good Boatswain, have care. Where's the
Master? Act like men.

BOATSWAIN I pray now, keep below.

ANTONIO Where is the Master, Boatswain?

BOATSWAIN Do you not hear him? You mar our
labour. Keep your cabins! You do assist the storm.

GONZALO Nay, good, be patient.

BOATSWAIN When the sea is. Hence! What care these
roarers for the name of king? To cabin! Silence!
Trouble us not.

GONZALO   Good, yet remember whom you have
   aboard.
BOATSWAIN   None that I more love than myself.
   You are a councillor. If you can command these
   elements to silence, and work the peace of the
   present, we will not hand a rope more. Use your
   authority. If you cannot, give thanks you have lived
   so long, and make yourself ready in your cabin for
   the mischance of the hour, if it so happens.—
   Cheerily, good hearts!—Out of our way, I say!   *Exit*
GONZALO   I have great comfort from this fellow. I
   think he has no drowning-mark upon him: his
   complexion is perfect gallows. Stand fast, good
   Fate, to his hanging. Make the rope of his destiny
   our cable, for our own is little advantage. If he is
   not born to be hanged, our case is miserable.
                   Exeunt Gonzalo and the other nobles

                   Enter BOATSWAIN

BOATSWAIN   Down with the topmast! Quick! Lower,
   lower! Bring her to try with main-course.

                   A cry within

A plague upon this howling! They are louder than
the weather, or our office.

                   Enter SEBASTIAN, ANTONIO, GONZALO

Yet again? What do you here? Shall we give over
and drown? Have you a mind to sink?
SEBASTIAN   A pox on your throat, you bawling,
   blasphemous, uncharitable dog!
BOATSWAIN   Work you, then.

ANTONIO   Hang, cur, hang, you insolent noisemaker!
We are less afraid to be drowned than you are.

GONZALO   I'll warrant him for drowning, though the
ship is no stronger than a nutshell and as leaky as
an unstanched wench.

BOATSWAIN   Lay her a-hold, a-hold! Set her two
courses! Off to sea again! Lay her off!

Enter Mariners wet

MARINERS   All lost! To prayers, to prayers! All lost!

Exeunt

BOATSWAIN   What, must our mouths be cold?

GONZALO
The King and Prince at prayers, let us assist them,
For our case is as theirs.

SEBASTIAN   I am out of patience.

ANTONIO
We are merely cheated of our lives by drunkards.
This wide-chapped rascal—would you might lie
drowning
The washing of ten tides!

GONZALO   He will be hanged yet,
Though every drop of water swears against it,
And gapes at widest to glut him.

    A confused noise within: 'Mercy on us!'—'We
split, we split!'—'Farewell, my wife and
children!'—'Farewell, brother!'—'We split, we
split, we split!'   *Exit Boatswain*

ANTONIO   Let us all sink with the King.

SEBASTIAN   Let us take leave of him.

Exit, with Antonio

GONZALO   Now would I give a thousand furlongs of sea
for an acre of barren ground. Long heath, brown
furze, anything. The wills above be done, but I
would rather die a dry death.   *Exit*

SCENE II
Before PROSPERO'S cell.

Enter PROSPERO *and* MIRANDA

MIRANDA
  If by your art, my dearest father, you have
  Put the wild waters in this roar, allay them.
  The sky it seems would pour down stinking pitch,
  But that the sea, mounting to the heaven's cheek,
  Dashes the fire out. O, I have suffered
  With those that I saw suffer! A brave vessel,
  Which had, no doubt, some noble creature in her,
  Dashed all to pieces. O, the cry did knock
  Against my very heart! Poor souls, they perished.
  Had I been any god of power, I would
  Have sunk the sea within the earth, before
  It should the good ship so have swallowed and
  The freighting souls within her.
PROSPERO   Be collected.
  No more amazement. Tell your piteous heart
  There's no harm done.
MIRANDA   O, woe the day!
PROSPERO   No harm.
  I have done nothing but in care of you,
  Of you, my dear one, you my daughter, who
  Are ignorant of what you are, naught knowing
  Of whence I am, nor that I am even better
  Than Prospero, master of a full poor cell,
  And your no greater father.
MIRANDA   More to know
  Did never meddle with my thoughts.
PROSPERO   It is time
  I should inform you farther. Lend your hand,
  And pluck my magic garment from me.—So,

Lie there, my art.—Wipe you your eyes. Have
   comfort.
The direful spectacle of the wreck, which touched
The very virtue of compassion in you,
I have with such provision in my art
So safely ordered, that there is no soul—
No, not so much perdition as a hair
Befallen any creature in the vessel
Which you heard cry, which you saw sink. Sit
   down.
For you must now know farther.

MIRANDA   You have often
Begun to tell me what I am, but stopped,
And left me to a fruitless inquisition,
Concluding, 'Stay: not yet.'

PROSPERO   The hour is now come.
The very minute bids you open your ear.
Obey, and be attentive. Can you remember
A time before we came unto this cell?
I do not think you can, for then you were not
Out three years old.

MIRANDA   Certainly, sir, I can.

PROSPERO

By what? By any other house or person?
Of any thing the image tells me, that
Has kept with your remembrance.

MIRANDA   It is far off,
And rather like a dream than an assurance
That my remembrance warrants. Had I not
Four or five women once that tended me?

PROSPERO

You had, and more, Miranda. But how is it
That this lives in your mind? What see you else
In the dark backward and abyss of time?
If you remember aught ere you came here,
How you came here you may.

MIRANDA   But that I do not.

PROSPERO

Twelve year since, Miranda, twelve year since,
Your father was the Duke of Milan and
A prince of power.

MIRANDA   Sir, are not you my father?

PROSPERO

Your mother was a piece of virtue, and
She said you were my daughter; and your father
Was Duke of Milan; and his only heir
And princess, no worse issued.

MIRANDA   O the heavens!

What foul play had we, that we came from thence?
Or blessed was it we did?

PROSPERO   Both, both, my girl.

By foul play, as you say, were we heaved thence,
But blessedly helped hither.

MIRANDA   O, my heart bleeds

To think of the grief that I have turned you to,
Now out of my remembrance! Please you, farther.

PROSPERO

My brother and your uncle, called Antonio—
I pray you mark me, that a brother should
Be so perfidious!—he, whom next yourself
Of all the world I loved, and to him put
The manage of my state. And at that time
Through all the signories it was the first;
And Prospero the prime duke, being so reputed
In dignity, and for the liberal arts
Without a parallel. Those being all my study,
The government I cast upon my brother,
And to my state grew stranger, being transported
And rapt in secret studies. Your false uncle—
Do you attend me?

MIRANDA   Sir, most heedfully.

PROSPERO

Being once perfected how to grant suits,
How to deny them, whom to advance, and whom
To check for over-topping, new created
The creatures that were mine, I say, or changed them,
Or else new formed them. Having both the key
Of officer and office, set all hearts in the state
To what tune pleased his ear, that now he was
The ivy which had hidden my princely trunk,
And sucked my verdure out of it. You attend not!

MIRANDA

O, good sir, I do.

PROSPERO   I pray you, mark me.

I, thus neglecting worldly ends, all dedicated
To closeness and the bettering of my mind
With that which—but by being so retired,
O'er-prized all popular rate—in my false brother
Awaked an evil nature. And my trust,
Like a good parent, did beget of him
A falsehood in its contrary, as great
As my trust was, which had indeed no limit,
A confidence boundless. He being thus lorded,
Not only with what my revenue yielded,
But what my power might else exact, like one
Who having unto truth, by telling of it,
Made such a sinner of his memory
To credit his own lie—he did believe
He was indeed the Duke, by substitution
And executing the outward face of royalty,
With all prerogative. Hence his ambition growing—
Do you hear?

MIRANDA   Your tale, sir, would cure deafness.

PROSPERO

To have no screen between this part he played
And him he played it for, he needs will be

    Absolute Milan. Me, poor man, my library
    Was dukedom large enough. Of temporal royalties
    He thinks me now incapable, confederates—
    So dry he was for sway—with the King of Naples
    To give him annual tribute, do him homage,
    Subject his coronet to his crown, and bend
    The dukedom yet unbowed—alas, poor Milan—
    To most ignoble stooping.

MIRANDA   O the heavens!

PROSPERO
    Mark his condition and the event; then tell me
    If this might be a brother.

MIRANDA   I should sin
    To think but nobly of my grandmother.
    Good wombs have borne bad sons.

PROSPERO   Now the condition.
    This King of Naples, being an enemy
    To me inveterate, hearkens to my brother's suit,
    Which was, that he—in lieu of the premises
    Of homage and I know not how much tribute—
    Should presently extirpate me and mine
    Out of the dukedom, and confer fair Milan,
    With all the honours, on my brother. Whereon,
    A treacherous army levied, one midnight
    Fated to the purpose, did Antonio open
    The gates of Milan; and, in the dead of darkness,
    The ministers for the purpose hurried thence
    Me and your crying self.

MIRANDA   Alas, for pity.
    I, not remembering how I cried out then,
    Will cry it over again. It is a hint
    That wrings my eyes to it.

PROSPERO   Hear a little further,
    And then I'll bring you to the present business
    Which now is upon us; without which, this story
    Were most impertinent.

MIRANDA   Wherefore did they not
  That hour destroy us?
PROSPERO   Well demanded, wench.
  My tale provokes that question. Dear, they durst not,
  So dear the love my people bore me; nor set
  A mark so bloody on the business, but
  With colours fairer painted their foul ends.
  In short, they hurried us aboard a bark,
  Bore us some leagues to sea, where they prepared
  A rotten carcass of a butt, not rigged,
  Nor tackle, sail, nor mast. The very rats
  Instinctively have quit it. There they hoist us,
  To cry to the sea that roared to us, to sigh
  To the winds, whose pity sighing back again
  Did us but loving wrong.
MIRANDA   Alas, what trouble
  Was I then to you!
PROSPERO   O, a cherubin
  You were that did preserve me. You did smile,
  Infusèd with a fortitude from heaven,
  When I have decked the sea with drops full salt,
  Under my burden groaned: which raised in me
  An undergoing stomach, to bear up
  Against what should ensue.
MIRANDA   How came we ashore?
PROSPERO
  By Providence divine.
  Some food we had, and some fresh water, that
  A noble Neapolitan, Gonzalo,
  Out of his charity—who being then appointed
  Master of this design—did give us; with
  Rich garments, linens, stuffs, and necessaries
  Which since have helped much. So, of his gentleness,
  Knowing I loved my books, he furnished me
  From my own library with volumes that
  I prize above my dukedom.

MIRANDA   Would I might
But ever see that man!

PROSPERO   Now I arise.
Sit still, and hear the last of our sea-sorrow.
Here in this island we arrived, and here
Have I, your schoolmaster, made you more profit
Than other princesses can, that have more time
For vainer hours, and tutors not so careful.

MIRANDA
Heaven thank you for it! Now, I pray you, sir,
For still 'tis beating in my mind, your reason
For raising this sea-storm?

PROSPERO   Know thus far forth.
By accident most strange, bountiful Fortune,
Now my dear lady, has my enemies
Brought to this shore. And by my prescience
I find my zenith does depend upon
A most auspicious star, whose influence
If now I court not, but omit, my fortunes
Will ever after droop. Here cease more questions.
You are inclined to sleep. It is a good dullness,
And give it way. I know you can not choose.

Miranda sleeps

Come away, servant, come! I am ready now.
Approach, my Ariel! Come!

Enter Ariel

ARIEL
All hail, great master! Grave sir, hail! I come
To answer your best pleasure, be it to fly,
To swim, to dive into the fire, to ride
On the curled clouds. To your strong bidding task
Ariel and all his quality.

PROSPERO   Have you, spirit,
  Performed to point the tempest that I bade you?
ARIEL
    To every article.
    I boarded the King's ship. Now on the beak,
    Now in the waist, the deck, in every cabin
    I flamed amazement. Sometimes I'd divide,
    And burn in many places. On the topmast,
    The yards, and bowsprit would I flame distinctly,
    Then meet and join Jove's lightnings, the precursors
    Of the dreadful thunderclaps, more momentary
    And sight-outrunning were not. The fire and cracks
    Of sulphurous roaring the most mighty Neptune
    Seem to besiege, and make his bold waves tremble,
    Yes, his dread trident shake.
PROSPERO   My brave spirit!
    Who was so firm, so constant, that this tumult
    Would not infect his reason?
ARIEL   Not a soul
    But felt a fever of the mad, and played
    Some tricks of desperation. All but mariners
    Plunged in the foaming brine, and quit the vessel,
    Then all afire with me. The King's son Ferdinand,
    With hair up-staring—then like reeds, not hair—
    Was the first man that leaped; cried, 'Hell is empty,
    And all the devils are here!'
PROSPERO   Why, that's my spirit!
    But was not this nigh shore?
ARIEL   Close by, my master.
PROSPERO
    But are they, Ariel, safe?
ARIEL   Not a hair perished.
    On their sustaining garments not a blemish,
    But fresher than before; and as you bade me,
    In troops I have dispersed them about the isle.
    The King's son have I landed by himself,

Whom I left cooling the air with sighs
In an odd angle of the isle, and sitting,
His arms in this sad knot.

PROSPERO   Of the King's ship,
The mariners, say how you have disposed,
And all the rest of the fleet?

ARIEL   Safely in harbour
Is the King's ship, in the deep nook where once
You called me up at midnight to fetch dew
From the ever-vexed Bermudas, there she's hid;
The mariners all under hatches stowed,
Who, with a charm joined to their suffered labour,
I have left asleep. And for the rest of the fleet,
Which I dispersed, they all have met again,
And are upon the Mediterranean flood
Bound sadly home for Naples,
Supposing that they saw the King's ship wrecked,
And his great person perish.

PROSPERO   Ariel, your charge
Exactly is performed, but there's more work.
What is the time of the day?

ARIEL   Past the mid-season.

PROSPERO
At least two glasses. The time between six and now
Must by us be spent most preciously.

ARIEL
Is there more toil? Since you do give me pains,
Let me remember you what you have promised,
Which is not yet performed me.

PROSPERO   How now? Moody?
What is it you can demand?

ARIEL   My liberty

PROSPERO
Before the time is out? No more.

ARIEL   I pray,
  Remember I have done you worthy service,
  Told you no lies, made you no mistakings, served
  Without grudge or grumblings. You did promise
  To abate me a full year.
PROSPERO   Do you forget
  From what a torment I did free you?
ARIEL   No.
PROSPERO
  You do; and think it much to tread the ooze
  Of the salt deep,
  To run upon the sharp wind of the north,
  To do me business in the veins of the earth
  When it is baked with frost.
ARIEL   I do not, sir.
PROSPERO
  You lie, malignant thing! Have you forgotten
  The foul witch Sycorax, who with age and envy
  Was grown into a hoop? Have you forgotten her?
ARIEL
  No, sir.
PROSPERO
        You have. Where was she born? Speak! Tell me!
ARIEL
  Sir, in Algiers.
PROSPERO   O, was she so! I must
  Once a month recount what you have been,
  Which you forget. This damned witch Sycorax,
  For mischiefs manifold, and sorceries terrible
  To enter human hearing, from Algiers,
  You know, was banished. For one thing she did
  They would not take her life. Is not this true?
ARIEL
  Ay, sir.

PROSPERO

This blue-eyed hag was hither brought with child,
And here was left by the sailors. You, my slave,
As you report yourself, was then her servant.
Because you were a spirit too delicate
To act her earthy and abhorred commands,
Refusing her behests, she did confine you,
By help of her more potent ministers,
And in her most unmitigable rage,
Into a cloven pine. Within which rift
Imprisoned, you did painfully remain
A dozen years; within which space she died,
And left you there, where you did vent your groans
As fast as millwheels strike. Then was this island—
Save for the son that she did litter here,
A freckled whelp, hag-born—not honoured with
A human shape.

ARIEL   Yes, Caliban her son.

PROSPERO

Dull thing, I say so! He, that Caliban
Whom now I keep in service. You best know
What torment I did find you in. Your groans
Did make wolves howl, and penetrate the breasts
Of ever-angry bears. It was a torment
To lay upon the damned, which Sycorax
Could not again undo. It was my art,
When I arrived and heard you, that made gape
The pine, and let you out.

ARIEL   I thank you, master.

PROSPERO

If you more murmur, I will rend an oak,
And peg you in its knotty entrails, till
You have howled away twelve winters.

ARIEL   Pardon, master.

I will be correspondent to command,
And do my spriting gently.

PROSPERO   Do so, and after two days
  I will discharge you.
ARIEL   That's my noble master!
  What shall I do? Say what! What shall I do?
PROSPERO
  Go make yourself like a nymph of the sea.
  Be subject to no sight but yours and mine, invisible
  To every eyeball else. Go take this shape,
  And hither come in it. Go! Hence with diligence!

                                     Exit Ariel

  Awake, dear heart, awake! You have slept well.
  Awake!
MIRANDA   The strangeness of your story put
  Heaviness in me.
PROSPERO   Shake it off. Come on;
  We'll visit Caliban, my slave, who never
  Yields us kind answer.
MIRANDA   It is a villain, sir,
  I do not love to look on.
PROSPERO   But, as it is,
  We cannot miss him. He does make our fire,
  Fetch in our wood, and serves in offices
  That profit us. What, ho! Slave! Caliban!
  You earth, you, speak!
CALIBAN (*within*)   There's wood enough within.
PROSPERO
  Come forth, I say! There's other business for you.
  Come, you tortoise! When?

          Enter ARIEL *like a water-nymph*

  Fine apparition! My quaint Ariel,
  Hark in your ear.
ARIEL   My lord, it shall be done.   *Exit*
PROSPERO
  You poisonous slave, got by the devil himself
  Upon your wicked dam, come forth!

Enter CALIBAN

CALIBAN
As wicked dew as ever my mother brushed
With raven's feather from unwholesome fen
Drop on you both. A south-west blow on you
And blister you all over.
PROSPERO
For this, be sure, tonight you shall have cramps,
Side-stitches that shall pen your breath up. Hedge-
hogs
Shall, for that vast of night that they may work,
All exercise on you. You shall be pinched
As thick as honey-comb, each pinch more stinging
Than bees that made them.
CALIBAN   I must eat my dinner.
This island's mine, by Sycorax my mother,
Which you take from me. When you came first,
You stroke me, and made much of me, would give
me
Water with berries in it, and teach me how
To name the bigger light, and how the less,
That burn by day and night. And then I loved you,
And showed you all the qualities of the isle,
The fresh springs, brine-pits, barren place and
fertile.
Cursèd be I that did so! All the charms
Of Sycorax—toads, beetles, bats light on you!
For I am all the subjects that you have,
Who first was my own king; and here you sty me
In this hard rock, while you do keep from me
The rest of the island.
PROSPERO   You most lying slave,
Whom stripes may move, not kindness! I have used
you,

Filth as you are, with human care, and lodged you
In my own cell, till you did seek to violate
The honour of my child.

CALIBAN

O ho, O ho! Would it had been done!
You did prevent me. I had peopled else
This isle with Calibans.

MIRANDA   Abhorrèd slave,
Which any print of goodness will not take,
Being capable of all ill! I pitied you,
Took pains to make you speak, taught you each
    hour
One thing or other. When you did not, savage,
Know your own meaning, but would gabble like
A thing most brutish, I endowed your purposes
With words that made them known. But your vile
    race,
Though you did learn, had that in it which good
    natures
Could not abide to be with. Therefore were you
Deservedly confined into this rock, who had
Deserved more than a prison.

CALIBAN

You taught me language, and my profit on it
Is, I know how to curse. The red plague rid you
For teaching me your language!

PROSPERO   Hag-seed, hence!
Fetch us in fuel—and be quick, you're best,
To answer other business. Shrug you, malice?
If you neglect, or do unwillingly
What I command, I'll rack you with old cramps,
Fill all your bones with aches and make you roar,
That beasts shall tremble at your din.

CALIBAN   No, pray you!
    (aside) I must obey. His art is of such power,

It would control my dam's god Setebos,
And make a vassal of him.

PROSPERO   So, slave. Hence!   *Exit Caliban*

Enter FERDINAND; *and* ARIEL, *invisible,*
playing and singing

ARIEL   *Song*
          Come unto these yellow sands,
              And then take hands.
          Curtsied when you have and kissed,
              The wild waves whist.
          Foot it featly here and there;
          And, sweet sprites, the burden bear.
              Hark, hark!
     (*Burden, dispersedly*) Bow-wow!
          The watch-dogs bark.
     (*Burden, dispersedly*) Bow-wow!
          Hark, hark! I hear
          The strain of strutting chanticleer
          Cry cock-a-diddle-dow!

FERDINAND
     Where should this music be? In the air or the earth?
     It sounds no more; and sure it waits upon
     Some god of the island. Sitting on a bank,
     Weeping again the King my father's wreck,
     This music crept by me upon the waters,
     Allaying both their fury and my passion
     With its sweet air. Thence I have followed it,
     Or it has drawn me, rather. But it is gone.
     No, it begins again.

ARIEL   *Song*
          Full fathom five your father lies,
              Of his bones are coral made;
          Those are pearls that were his eyes;

      Nothing of him that does fade,
      But does suffer a sea-change
      Into something rich and strange.
      Sea-nymphs hourly ring his knell:
(*Burden*) Ding-dong.
      Hark! Now I hear them—Ding-dong bell.

FERDINAND
  The ditty does remember my drowned father.
  This is no mortal business, nor any sound
  That the earth owns. I hear it now above me.

PROSPERO
  The fringèd curtains of your eye advance,
  And say what you see yonder.

MIRANDA   What? A spirit?
  Lord, how it looks about! Believe me, sir,
  It carries a brave form. But it is a spirit.

PROSPERO
  No, wench. It eats and sleeps and has such senses
  As we have, such. This gallant whom you see
  Was in the wreck; and, though he's somewhat stained
  With grief, that's beauty's canker, you might call
    him
  A goodly person. He has lost his fellows,
  And strays about to find them.

MIRANDA   I might call him
  A thing divine, for nothing natural
  I ever saw so noble.

PROSPERO (*aside*)   It goes on, I see,
  As my soul prompts it.—Spirit, fine spirit, I'll free
    you
  Within two days for this!

FERDINAND   Most sure, the goddess
  On whom these airs attend! Grant that my prayer
  May know if you remain upon this island,
  And that you will some good instruction give

How I may bear me here. My prime request,
Which I do last pronounce, is—O you wonder!—
If you are maid or no?

MIRANDA   No wonder, sir,
But certainly a maid.

FERDINAND   My language? Heavens!
I am the best of them that speak this speech,
Were I but where it is spoken.

PROSPERO   How? The best?
What were you if the King of Naples heard you?

FERDINAND
A single thing, as I am now, that wonders
To hear you speak of Naples. He does hear me,
And that he does, I weep. Myself am Naples,
Who with my eyes, never since at ebb, beheld
The King my father wrecked.

MIRANDA   Alas, for mercy!

FERDINAND
Yes, faith, and all his lords, the Duke of Milan
And his brave son being two.

PROSPERO (*aside*)   The Duke of Milan
And his still braver daughter could control you,
If now it were fit to do it. At the first sight
They have changed eyes. Delicate Ariel,
I'll set you free for this.—A word, good sir.
I fear you have done yourself some wrong. A word!

MIRANDA
Why speaks my father so ungently? This
Is the third man that ever I saw; the first
That ever I sighed for. Pity move my father
To be inclined my way.

FERDINAND   O, if a virgin,
And your affection not gone forth, I'll make you
The Queen of Naples.

PROSPERO   Soft, sir! One word more.
   (aside) They are both in either's powers. But this
     swift business
   I must uneasy make, lest too light winning
   Makes the prize light.—One word more! I charge
     you
   That you attend me. You do here usurp
   The name you own not, and have put yourself
   Upon this island as a spy, to win it
   From me, the lord of it.
FERDINAND   No, as I am a man!
MIRANDA
   There's nothing ill can dwell in such a temple.
   If the ill spirit has so fair a house,
   Good things will strive to dwell with it.
PROSPERO   Follow me.
   (to Miranda) Speak not you for him. He's a traitor.—
     Come!
   I'll manacle your neck and feet together.
   Sea-water shall you drink; your food shall be
   The fresh-brook mussels, withered roots, and husks
   Wherein the acorn cradled. Follow!
FERDINAND   No!
   I will resist such entertainment till
   My enemy has more power.

       He draws, and is charmed from moving

MIRANDA   O dear father,
   Make not too rash a trial of him, for
   He's noble, and not fearful.
PROSPERO   What, I say,
   My foot my tutor?—Put your sword up, traitor,

Who make a show, but dare not strike, your
   conscience
Is so possessed with guilt. Come from your ward!
For I can here disarm you with this stick,
And make your weapon drop.

MIRANDA   Beseech you, father!

PROSPERO

Hence! Hang not on my garments.

MIRANDA   Sir, have pity.
I'll be his surety.

PROSPERO   Silence! One word more
Shall make me chide you, if not hate you. What,
An advocate for an impostor? Hush!
You think there are no more such shapes as he,
Having seen but him and Caliban. Foolish wench!
To the most of men this is a Caliban,
And they to him are angels.

MIRANDA   My affections
Are then most humble. I have no ambition
To see a goodlier man.

PROSPERO   Come on, obey!
Your nerves are in their infancy again,
And have no vigour in them.

FERDINAND   So they are.
My spirits, as in a dream, are all bound up.
My father's loss, the weakness which I feel,
The wreck of all my friends, and this man's threats
To whom I am subdued, are but light to me,
Might I but through my prison once a day
Behold this maid. All corners else of the earth
Let liberty make use of. Space enough
Have I in such a prison.

PROSPERO *(aside)*   It works. *(to Ferdinand)* Come on.—
You have done well, fine Ariel! *(to Ferdinand)*
   Follow me. *(to Ariel)*
Hark what you else shall do me.

MIRANDA   Be of comfort.
  My father's of a better nature, sir,
  Than he appears by speech. This is unwonted
  Which now came from him.
PROSPERO *(to Ariel)*   You shall be as free
  As mountain winds; but then exactly do
  All points of my command.
ARIEL   To the syllable.
PROSPERO
  Come, follow! *(to Miranda)* Speak not for him.
                              Exeunt

Act II

SCENE I
Another part of the island.

Enter ALONSO, SEBASTIAN, ANTONIO, GONZALO,
ADRIAN, FRANCISCO, *and others*

GONZALO
  Beseech you, sir, be merry. You have cause—
  So have we all—of joy; for our escape
  Is much beyond our loss. Our hint of woe
  Is common. Every day, some sailor's wife,
  The masters of some merchant, and the merchant,
  Have just our theme of woe. But for the miracle,
  I mean our preservation, few in millions
  Can speak like us. Then wisely, good sir, weigh
  Our sorrow with our comfort.

ALONSO   Pray you, peace.

SEBASTIAN *(aside to Antonio)* He receives comfort
  like cold porridge.

ANTONIO *(aside to Sebastian)* The visitor will not
  give him over so.

SEBASTIAN *(aside to Antonio)* Look, he's winding up
  the watch of his wit. By and by it will strike.

GONZALO Sir—

SEBASTIAN One: tell.

GONZALO
  When every grief is entertained, what's offered
  Comes to the entertainer—

SEBASTIAN A dollar.

GONZALO Dolour comes to him indeed. You have
  spoken truer than you purposed.

SEBASTIAN You have taken it wiselier than I meant
  you should.

GONZALO *(to Alonso)* Therefore, my lord—

ANTONIO Fie, what a spendthrift is he of his tongue!

ALONSO I pray you, spare.

GONZALO Well, I have done. But yet—

SEBASTIAN He will be talking.

ANTONIO Which, of he or Adrian, for a good wager,
  first begins to crow?

SEBASTIAN The old cock.

ANTONIO The cockerel.

SEBASTIAN Done. The wager?

ANTONIO A laughter.

SEBASTIAN A match.

ADRIAN Though this island seems to be desert—

ANTONIO Ha, ha, ha!

SEBASTIAN So, you're paid.

ADRIAN Uninhabitable, and almost inaccessible—

SEBASTIAN Yet—

ADRIAN Yet—

ANTONIO He could not miss it.

ADRIAN   It must needs be of subtle, tender, and
delicate temperance.

ANTONIO   Temperance was a delicate wench.

SEBASTIAN   Ay, and a subtle, as he most learnedly
delivered.

ADRIAN   The air breathes upon us here most sweetly.

SEBASTIAN   As if it had lungs, and rotten ones.

ANTONIO   Or, as though perfumed by a fen.

GONZALO   Here is everything advantageous to life.

ANTONIO   True, save means to live.

SEBASTIAN   Of that there's none, or little.

GONZALO   How lush and lusty the grass looks! How
green!

ANTONIO   The ground, indeed, is tawny.

SEBASTIAN   With an eye of green in it.

ANTONIO   He misses not much.

SEBASTIAN   No. He does but mistake the truth totally.

GONZALO   But the rarity of it is—which is indeed
almost beyond credit—

SEBASTIAN   As many vouched rarities are.

GONZALO   That our garments being, as they were,
drenched in the sea hold, notwithstanding, their
freshness and glosses; being rather new-dyed than
stained with salt water.

ANTONIO   If but one of his pockets could speak, would
it not say he lies?

SEBASTIAN   Ay, or very falsely pocket up his report.

GONZALO   It seems our garments are now as fresh as
when we put them on first in Africa, at the
marriage of the King's fair daughter Claribel to the
King of Tunis.

SEBASTIAN   It was a sweet marriage, and we prosper
well in our return.

ADRIAN   Tunis was never graced before with such a
paragon to their queen.

GONZALO   Not since widow Dido's time.

ANTONIO   Widow? A pox on that! How came that
   widow in? Widow Dido!

SEBASTIAN   What if he had said 'widower Aeneas' too?
   Good Lord, how you take it!

ADRIAN   'Widow Dido', said you? You make me
   study of that. She was of Carthage, not of Tunis.

GONZALO   This Tunis, sir, was Carthage.

ADRIAN   Carthage?

GONZALO   I assure you, Carthage.

ANTONIO   His word is more than the miraculous harp.

SEBASTIAN   He has raised the wall, and houses too.

ANTONIO   What impossible matter will he make easy
   next?

SEBASTIAN   I think he will carry this island home in
   his pocket and give it his son for an apple.

ANTONIO   And sowing the kernels of it in the sea,
   bring forth more islands.

GONZALO   Ay.

ANTONIO   Why, in good time.

GONZALO   (to Alonso) Sir, we were talking, that our
   garments seem now as fresh as when we were at
   Tunis at the marriage of your daughter, who is now
   Queen.

ANTONIO   And the rarest that ever came there.

SEBASTIAN   Except, I beseech you, widow Dido.

ANTONIO   O, widow Dido? Ay, widow Dido.

GONZALO   Is not, sir, my doublet as fresh as the first
   day I wore it? I mean, in a sort.

ANTONIO   That 'sort' was well fished for.

GONZALO   When I wore it at your daughter's
   marriage.

ALONSO
   You cram these words into my ears against
   The stomach of my sense. Would I had never
   Married my daughter there! For, coming thence,

My son is lost and, in my rate, she too,
Who is so far from Italy removed
I never again shall see her. O you my heir
Of Naples and of Milan, what strange fish
Has made his meal on you?

FRANCISCO   Sir, he may live.
I saw him beat the surges under him,
And ride upon their backs. He trod the water,
Whose enmity he flung aside, and breasted
The surge most swollen that met him. His bold head
Above the contentious waves he kept, and oared
Himself with his good arms in lusty stroke
To the shore, that o'er his wave-worn basis bowed,
As stooping to relieve him. I do not doubt
He came alive to land.

ALONSO   No, no, he's gone.

SEBASTIAN
Sir, you may thank yourself for this great loss,
That would not bless our Europe with your
    daughter,
But rather loose her to an African,
Where she, at least, is banished from your eye,
Who has cause to wet the grief of it.

ALONSO   Pray, peace.

SEBASTIAN
You were kneeled to and importuned otherwise
By all of us; and the fair soul herself
Weighed between loathness and obedience at
Which end of the beam should bow. We have lost
    your son,
I fear, for ever. Milan and Naples have
More widows in them of this business' making
Than we bring men to comfort them.
The fault's your own.

ALONSO   So is the dearest of the loss.

GONZALO
  My lord Sebastian,
  The truth you speak does lack some gentleness,
  And time to speak it in. You rub the sore,
  When you should bring the plaster.
SEBASTIAN   Very well.
ANTONIO   And most surgically.
GONZALO   *(to Alonso)*
  It is foul weather in us all, good sir,
  When you are cloudy.
SEBASTIAN   *(aside to Antonio)*
                           Foul weather?
ANTONIO   *(aside to Sebastian)*   Very foul.
GONZALO
  Had I plantation of this isle, my lord—
ANTONIO   *(aside to Sebastian)*
  He'd sow it with nettle-seed.
SEBASTIAN   *(aside to Antonio)* Or docks, or mallows.
GONZALO
  And were the king of it, what would I do?
SEBASTIAN   *(aside to Antonio)* Escape being drunk, for
  want of wine.
GONZALO
  In the commonwealth I would by contraries
  Execute all things. For no kind of traffic
  Would I admit, no name of magistrate.
  Letters should not be known. Riches, poverty,
  And use of service, none. Contract, succession,
  Boundaries of land, tilth, vineyard, none.
  No use of metal, corn, or wine, or oil.
  No occupation: all men idle, all,
  And women too, but innocent and pure.
  No sovereignty—
SEBASTIAN   *(aside to Antonio)* Yet he would be king of
  it.

ANTONIO   *(aside to Sebastian)* The latter end of his
commonwealth forgets the beginning.

GONZALO

All things in common nature should produce
Without sweat or endeavour. Treason, felony,
Sword, pike, knife, gun, or need of any engine
Would I not have. But nature should bring forth
Of its own kind all plenty, all abundance,
To feed my innocent people.

SEBASTIAN   *(aside to Antonio)* No marrying among his
subjects?

ANTONIO   *(aside to Sebastian)* None, man, all idle—
whores and knaves.

GONZALO

I would with such perfection govern, sir,
To excel the Golden Age.

SEBASTIAN   'Save his majesty!

ANTONIO

Long live Gonzalo!

GONZALO   And—do you mark me, sir?

ALONSO

Pray, no more. You do talk nothing to me.

GONZALO   I do well believe your highness, and did it
to minister occasion to these gentlemen, who are of
such sensible and nimble lungs that they always
use to laugh at nothing.

ANTONIO   It was you we laughed at.

GONZALO   Who, in this kind of merry fooling, am
nothing to you; so you may continue, and laugh at
nothing still.

ANTONIO   What a blow was there given!

SEBASTIAN   If it had not fallen flat-long.

GONZALO   You are gentlemen of brave mettle. You
would lift the moon out of her sphere, if she would
continue in it five weeks without changing.

Enter ARIEL, *playing solemn music*

SEBASTIAN   We would so, and then go a-bat-fowling.
ANTONIO   Nay, good my lord, be not angry.
GONZALO   No, I warrant you, I will not adventure my
   discretion so weakly. Will you laugh me asleep, for
   I am very heavy?
ANTONIO   Go sleep, and hear us.

All sleep except ALONSO, SEBASTIAN, *and* ANTONIO

ALONSO
   What, all so soon asleep? I wish my eyes
   Would, with themselves, shut up my thoughts. I
      find
   They are inclined to do so.
SEBASTIAN   Please you, sir,
   Do not omit the heavy offer of it.
   It seldom visits sorrow; when it does,
   It is a comforter.
ANTONIO   We two, my lord,
   Will guard your person while you take your rest,
   And watch your safety.
ALONSO   Thank you. Wondrous heavy.
                        Alonso sleeps. Exit Ariel

SEBASTIAN
   What a strange drowsiness possesses them!
ANTONIO
   It is the quality of the climate.
SEBASTIAN   Why
   Does it not then that our eyelids sink? I find
   Not myself disposed to sleep.
ANTONIO
   Nor I. My spirits are nimble.
   They fell together all, as by consent.

They dropped, as by a thunderstroke. What might,
Worthy Sebastian?—O, what might?—No more!
And yet I think I see it in your face,
What you should be. The occasion speaks you, and
My strong imagination sees a crown
Dropping upon your head.

SEBASTIAN   What, are you waking?

ANTONIO
Do you not hear me speak?

SEBASTIAN   I do, and surely
It is a sleepy language, and you speak
Out of your sleep. What is it you did say?
This is a strange repose, to be asleep
With eyes wide open; standing, speaking, moving,
And yet so fast asleep.

ANTONIO   Noble Sebastian,
You let your fortune sleep—die, rather; wink
While you are waking.

SEBASTIAN   You do snore distinctly.
There's meaning in your snores.

ANTONIO
I am more serious than my custom. You
Must be so too, if heed me; which to do
Trebles you over.

SEBASTIAN   Well, I am standing water.

ANTONIO
I'll teach you how to flow.

SEBASTIAN   Do so. To ebb
Hereditary sloth instructs me.

ANTONIO   O,
If you but knew how you the purpose cherish
While thus you mock it! How, in stripping it,
You more invest it! Ebbing men, indeed,
Most often do so near the bottom run
By their own fear, or sloth.

SEBASTIAN   Pray you, say on.
   The setting of your eye and cheek proclaim
   A matter from you; and a birth, indeed,
   Which pains you much to yield.

ANTONIO   Thus, sir:
   Although this lord of weak remembrance, this,
   Who shall be of as little memory
   When he is earthed, has here almost persuaded—
   For he's a spirit of persuasion, only
   Professes to persuade—the King his son's alive,
   'Tis as impossible that he's undrowned
   As he that sleeps here swims.

SEBASTIAN   I have no hope
   That he's undrowned.

ANTONIO   O, out of that no hope
   What great hope have you! No hope that way is
   Another way so high a hope that even
   Ambition cannot pierce a wink beyond,
   But doubt discovery there. Will you grant with me
   That Ferdinand is drowned?

SEBASTIAN   He's gone.

ANTONIO   Then, tell me,
   Who's the next heir of Naples?

SEBASTIAN   Claribel.

ANTONIO
   She that is Queen of Tunis; she that dwells
   Ten leagues beyond man's life. She that from Naples
   Can have no note, unless the sun were post—
   The Man in the Moon's too slow—till newborn
     chins
   Be rough and razorable. She that from whom
   We all were sea-swallowed, though some cast again
   And, by that destiny, to perform an act
   Whereof what's past is prologue, what to come,
   In yours and my discharge.

SEBASTIAN   What stuff is this?
  How say you?
  'Tis true my brother's daughter is Queen of Tunis,
  So is she heir of Naples, between which regions
  There is some space.
ANTONIO   A space whose every cubit
  Seems to cry out, 'How shall that Claribel
  Measure us back to Naples? Keep in Tunis,
  And let Sebastian wake.' Say this were death
  That now has seized them, why, they were no worse
  Than now they are. There are that can rule Naples
  As well as he that sleeps; lords that can prate
  As amply and unnecessarily
  As this Gonzalo. I myself could make
  A chough of as deep chat. O, that you bore
  The mind that I do! What a sleep were this
  For your advancement! Do you understand me?
SEBASTIAN
  I think I do.
ANTONIO   And how does your content
  Tender your own good fortune?
SEBASTIAN   I remember
  You did supplant your brother Prospero.
ANTONIO   True.
  And look how well my garments sit upon me,
  Much better than before. My brother's servants
  Were then my fellows. Now they are my men.
SEBASTIAN
  But, for your conscience?
ANTONIO
  Ay, sir, where lies that? If it were a corn,
  It would put me to my slipper; but I feel not
  This deity in my bosom. Twenty consciences
  That stand between me and Milan, candied be they,
  And melt ere they molest. Here lies your brother,

No better than the earth he lies upon,
If he were that which now he's like—that's dead—
Whom I with this obedient steel, three inches of it,
Can lay to bed for ever. While you, doing thus,
To the perpetual wink for aye might put
This ancient morsel, this Sir Prudence, who
Should not upbraid our course. For all the rest,
They'll take suggestion as a cat laps milk.
They'll tell the clock to any business that
We say befits the hour.

SEBASTIAN   Your case, dear friend,
Shall be my precedent. As you got Milan,
I'll come by Naples. Draw your sword. One stroke
Shall free you from the tribute which you pay,
And I the King shall love you.

ANTONIO   Draw together.
And when I rear my hand, do you the like,
To aim it on Gonzalo.

SEBASTIAN   O, but one word.

Enter ARIEL *with music and song*

ARIEL
My master through his art foresees the danger
That you, his friend, are in, and sends me forth—
For else his project dies—to keep them living.

Sings in GONZALO'S *ear*

While you here do snoring lie,
Open-eyed conspiracy
  His time does take.
If of life you keep a care,
Shake off slumber, and beware.
  Awake, awake!

ANTONIO
  Then let us both be sudden.
GONZALO *(awakes)*   Now, good angels
  Preserve the King!

                        The others awake

ALONSO
  Why, how now?—Ho, awake!—Why are you drawn?
  Wherefore this ghastly looking?
GONZALO   What's the matter?
SEBASTIAN
  While we stood here securing your repose,
  Even now, we heard a hollow burst of bellowing
  Like bulls, or rather lions. Did it not awake you?
  It struck my ear most terribly.
ALONSO   I heard nothing.
ANTONIO
  O, it was a din to fright a monster's ear,
  To make an earthquake! Sure it was the roar
  Of a whole herd of lions.
ALONSO   Heard you this, Gonzalo?
GONZALO
  Upon my honour, sir, I heard a humming,
  And that a strange one too, which did awake me.
  I shaked you, sir, and cried. As my eyes opened,
  I saw their weapons drawn. There was a noise,
  That's verily. 'Tis best we stand upon our guard,
  Or that we quit this place. Let's draw our weapons.
ALONSO
  Lead off this ground and let's make further search
  For my poor son.
GONZALO   Heavens keep him from these beasts!
  For he is sure in the island.
ALONSO   Lead away.

ARIEL
Prospero my lord shall know what I have done.
So, King, go safely on to seek your son.   *Exeunt*

SCENE II
Another part of the island.

Enter CALIBAN *with a burden of wood. Thunder.*

CALIBAN
All the infections that the sun sucks up
From bogs, fens, flats, on Prospero fall; make him
By inches a disease! His spirits hear me,
And yet I needs must curse. But they'll nor pinch,
Fright me with hedgehogs, pitch me in the mire,
Nor lead me, like a firebrand, in the dark
Out of my way, unless he bids them. But
For every trifle are they set upon me;
Sometimes like apes, that mow and chatter at me,
And after bite me; then like hedgehogs, which
Lie tumbling in my barefoot way, and mount
Their pricks at my footfall. Sometimes am I
All wound with adders, who with cloven tongues
Do hiss me into madness.

Enter TRINCULO

                              Lo, now, lo!
Here comes a spirit of his, and to torment me
For bringing wood in slowly. I'll fall flat.
Perchance he will not mind me.
TRINCULO Here's neither bush nor shrub, to bear off
any weather at all, and another storm brewing. I
hear it sing in the wind. Yon same black cloud, yon

huge one, looks like a foul barrel that would shed
its liquor. If it should thunder as it did before, I
know not where to hide my head. Yon same cloud
cannot choose but fall by pailfuls. What have we
here? A man or a fish? Dead or alive? A fish! He
smells like a fish; a very ancient and fishlike smell;
a kind of not-of-the-newest salt-hake. A strange
fish! Were I in England now, as once I was, and had
but this fish painted, not a holiday fool there but
would give a piece of silver. There would this
monster make a man. Any strange beast there
makes a man. When they will not give a penny to
relieve a lame beggar, they will lay out ten to see a
dead Indian. Legged like a man! And his fins like
arms! Warm, on my faith! I do now let loose my
opinion, hold it no longer. This is no fish, but an
islander that has lately suffered by a thunderbolt.

Thunder

Alas, the storm is come again. My best way is to
creep under his cloak. There is no shelter
hereabout. Misery acquaints a man with strange
bed-fellows. I will here shroud till the dregs of the
storm are past.

Enter STEPHANO, *singing, a bottle in his hand.*

STEPHANO
      I shall no more to sea, to sea,
        Here shall I die ashore.
This is a very scurvy tune to sing at a man's funeral.
Well, here's my comfort.

He drinks and then sings

The master, the swabber, the boatswain, and I,
The gunner and his mate,
Loved Mall, Meg, and Marian, and Margery,
But none of us cared for Kate.
For she had a tongue with a tang,
Would cry to a sailor, 'Go hang!'
She loved not the savour of tar nor of pitch,
Yet a tailor might scratch her where'ere she did
itch.
Then to sea boys, and let her go hang!
This is a scurvy tune too. But here's my comfort.

He drinks

CALIBAN Do not torment me! O!

STEPHANO What's the matter? Have we devils here?
Do you put tricks upon us with savages and men of
the Indies, ha? I have not escaped drowning to be
afraid now of your four legs. For it has been said,
'As proper a man as ever went on four legs cannot
make him give ground'; and it shall be said so
again, while Stephano breathes at his nostrils.

CALIBAN The spirit torments me! O!

STEPHANO This is some monster of the isle with four
legs, and who has got, as I take it, an ague. Where
the devil should he learn our language? I will give
him some relief, if it is but for that. If I can recover
him, and keep him tame, and get to Naples with
him, he's a present for any emperor that ever trod
on calves' leather.

CALIBAN Do not torment me, pray. I'll bring my
wood home faster.

STEPHANO He's in his fit now, and does not talk after
the wisest. He shall taste of my bottle. If he has
never drunk wine before, it will go near to remove
his fit. If I can recover him, and keep him tame, I

will not take too much for him. He shall pay for
him that has him, and that soundly.

CALIBAN   You do me yet but little hurt. You will soon.
I know it by your trembling. Now Prosper works
upon you.

STEPHANO   Come on your ways. Open your mouth.
Here is that which will give language to you, cat.
Open your mouth. This will shake your shaking, I
can tell you, and that soundly. (*He gives Caliban
wine*) You cannot tell who's your friend. Open your
chaps again.

TRINCULO   I should know that voice. It should be—
but he is drowned, and these are devils. O, defend
me!

STEPHANO   Four legs and two voices—a most delicate
monster. His forward voice now is to speak well of
his friend. His backward voice is to utter foul
speeches and to detract. If all the wine in my bottle
will recover him, I will help his ague. Come!
(*Caliban drinks*) Amen! I will pour some in your
other mouth.

TRINCULO   Stephano!

STEPHANO   Does your other mouth call me? Mercy,
mercy! This is a devil, and no monster. I will leave
him; I have no long spoon.

TRINCULO   Stephano! If you are Stephano, touch me
and speak to me; for I am Trinculo—be not afraid—
your good friend Trinculo.

STEPHANO   If you are Trinculo, come forth. I'll pull
you by the lesser legs. If any are Trinculo's legs,
these are they. You are very Trinculo indeed! How
came you to be the seat of this mooncalf? Can he
vent Trinculos?

TRINCULO   I took him to be killed with a
thunderstroke. But are you not drowned, Stephano?
I hope now you are not drowned. Is the storm

overblown? I hid me under the dead mooncalf's
cloak for fear of the storm. And are you living,
Stephano? O Stephano, two Neapolitans escaped?

STEPHANO   Pray, do not turn me about. My stomach
is not constant.

CALIBAN   *(aside)*
These are fine things, if they are not sprites.
That's a brave god, and bears celestial liquor.
I will kneel to him.

STEPHANO   How did you escape? How came you
hither? Swear by this bottle how you came hither. I
escaped upon a butt of sack, which the sailors
heaved overboard, by this bottle, which I made of
the bark of a tree, and my own hands, since I was
cast ashore.

CALIBAN   I'll swear upon that bottle to be your true
subject, for the liquor is not earthly.

STEPHANO   Here! Swear, then, how you escaped.

TRINCULO   Swam ashore, man, like a duck. I can
swim like a duck, I'll be sworn.

STEPHANO   Here, kiss the book. *(He gives him wine)*
Though you can swim like a duck, you are made
like a goose.

TRINCULO   O Stephano, got any more of this?

STEPHANO   The whole butt, man. My cellar is in a
rock by the seaside, where my wine is hid. How
now, mooncalf? How does your ague?

CALIBAN   Have you not dropped from heaven?

STEPHANO   Out of the moon, I do assure you. I was
the Man in the Moon when time was.

CALIBAN   I have seen you in her, and I do adore you.
My mistress showed me you, and your dog, and
your bush.

STEPHANO   Come, swear to that. Kiss the book. I will
furnish it soon with new contents. Swear! *(CALIBAN
drinks)*

TRINCULO By this good light, this is a very shallow
  monster! I afraid of him? A very weak monster! The
  Man in the Moon? A most poor credulous
  monster!—Well drawn, monster, in good faith!
CALIBAN I'll show you every fertile inch of the
  island, and I will kiss your foot. I pray you, be my
  god.
TRINCULO By this light, a most perfidious and
  drunken monster! When his god's asleep, he'll rob
  his bottle.
CALIBAN I'll kiss your foot. I'll swear myself your
  subject.
STEPHANO Come on then. Down, and swear!
TRINCULO I shall laugh myself to death at this puppy-
  headed monster. A most scurvy monster! I could
  find in my heart to beat him—
STEPHANO Come, kiss.
TRINCULO But that the poor monster's in drink. An
  abominable monster!
CALIBAN

  I'll show you the best springs. I'll pluck you berries.
  I'll fish for you, and get you wood enough.
  A plague upon the tyrant that I serve!
  I'll bear him no more sticks, but follow you,
  You wondrous man.
TRINCULO A most ridiculous monster, to make a
  wonder of a poor drunkard!
CALIBAN

  I pray you, let me bring you where apples grow;
  And I with my long nails will dig you pig-nuts,
  Show you a jay's nest, and instruct you how
  To snare the nimble marmoset. I'll bring you
  To clustering filberts, and sometimes I'll get you
  Young mussels from the rock. Will you go with me?
STEPHANO I pray now, lead the way without any
  more talking.—Trinculo, the King and all our

company else being drowned, we will inherit here.
Here, bear my bottle. Fellow Trinculo, we'll fill
him by and by again.

CALIBAN *sings drunkenly*

CALIBAN Farewell, master! Farewell, farewell!
TRINCULO A howling monster! A drunken monster!
CALIBAN
     No more dams I'll make for fish,
       Nor fetch in firing
     At requiring,
     Nor scrape trenchering, nor wash dish.
       Ban, Ban, Ca-Caliban
       Has a new master—get a new man!
Freedom, high-day! High-day, freedom! Freedom,
high-day, freedom!
STEPHANO O brave monster! Lead the way.   *Exeunt*

Act III

SCENE I
Before PROSPERO'S cell.

Enter FERDINAND, *bearing a log*

FERDINAND
  There are some sports are painful, and their labour
  Delight in them sets off. Some kinds of baseness
  Are nobly undergone, and most poor matters
  Point to rich ends. This my mean task

Would be as heavy to me as odious, but
The mistress whom I serve quickens what's dead,
And makes my labours pleasures. O, she is
Ten times more gentle than her father's crabbed,
And he's composed of harshness. I must remove
Some thousands of these logs and pile them up,
Upon a sore injunction. My sweet mistress
Weeps when she sees me work, and says such
    baseness
Had never like executor. I forget;
But these sweet thoughts do even refresh my
    labours,
Most busy, lest when I do it.

Enter MIRANDA, *and* PROSPERO *at a distance, unseen*

MIRANDA   Alas, now pray you
Work not so hard. I would the lightning had
Burnt up those logs that you are enjoined to pile!
Pray, set it down and rest you. When this burns,
It will weep for having wearied you. My father
Is hard at study. Pray now, rest yourself.
He's safe for these three hours.
FERDINAND   O most dear mistress,
The sun will set before I shall discharge
What I must strive to do.
MIRANDA   If you'll sit down,
I'll bear your logs the while. Pray, give me that.
I'll carry it to the pile.
FERDINAND   No, precious creature.
I had rather crack my sinews, break my back,
Than you should such dishonour undergo,
While I sit lazy by.
MIRANDA   It would become me
As well as it does you; and I should do it

With much more ease; for my good will is to it,
And yours it is against.
PROSPERO   *(aside)*   Poor worm, you are infected.
  This visitation shows it.
MIRANDA   You look wearily.
FERDINAND
  No, noble mistress, it is fresh morning with me
  When you are by at night. I do beseech you,
  Chiefly that I might set it in my prayers,
  What is your name?
MIRANDA   Miranda. O my father,
  I have broken your behest to say so!
FERDINAND   Admired Miranda!
  Indeed, the top of admiration, worth
  What is dearest to the world. Full many a lady
  I have eyed with best regard, and many a time
  The harmony of their tongues has into bondage
  Brought my too diligent ear. For several virtues
  Have I liked several women; never any
  With so full soul but some defect in her
  Did quarrel with the noblest grace she owned,
  And put it to defeat. But you, O you,
  So perfect and so peerless, are created
  Of every creature's best.
MIRANDA   I do not know
  One of my sex; no woman's face remember,
  Save, from my glass, my own. Nor have I seen
  More that I may call men than you, good friend,
  And my dear father. How features are abroad
  I am skill-less of; but, by my chastity,
  The jewel in my dower, I would not wish
  Any companion in the world but you.
  Nor can imagination form a shape,
  Besides yourself, to like of. But I prattle
  Something too wildly, and my father's precepts
  I therein do forget.

FERDINAND   I am, in my condition,
  A prince, Miranda; I do think, a king—
  I would not so—and would no more endure
  This wooden slavery than to suffer
  The flesh-fly blow my mouth. Hear my soul speak.
  The very instant that I saw you did
  My heart fly to your service, there resides
  To make me slave to it; and for your sake
  Am I this patient log-man.
MIRANDA   Do you love me?
FERDINAND
  O heaven, O earth, bear witness to this sound,
  And crown what I profess with kind event,
  If I speak true! If hollowly, invert
  What best is boded me to mischief! I,
  Beyond all limit of what else in the world,
  Do love, prize, honour you.
MIRANDA   I am a fool
  To weep at what I am glad of.
PROSPERO   (aside)   Fair encounter
  Of two most rare affections. Heavens rain grace
  On that which breeds between them.
FERDINAND   Wherefore weep you?
MIRANDA
  At my unworthiness, that dares not offer
  What I desire to give, and much less take
  What I shall die to want. But this is trifling;
  And all the more it seeks to hide itself,
  The bigger bulk it shows. Hence, bashful cunning!
  And prompt me, plain and holy innocence.
  I am your wife, if you will marry me.
  If not, I'll die your maid. To be your fellow
  You may deny me, but I'll be your servant
  Whether you will or no.
FERDINAND   My mistress, dearest,
  And I thus humble ever.

MIRANDA   My husband, then?

FERDINAND

Ay, with a heart as willing
As bondage ever of freedom. Here's my hand.

MIRANDA

And mine, with my heart in it; and now farewell
Till half an hour hence.

FERDINAND   A thousand, thousand!

Exeunt Ferdinand and Miranda in different directions.

PROSPERO

So glad of this as they I cannot be,
Who are surprised with all, but my rejoicing
At nothing can be more. I'll to my book,
For yet ere suppertime must I perform
Much business appertaining.   *Exit*

SCENE II
Another part of the island.

Enter CALIBAN, STEPHANO, *and* TRINCULO

STEPHANO   Tell not me! When the butt is out we will
drink water; not a drop before. Therefore, bear up
and board them. Servant monster, drink to me.

TRINCULO   Servant monster? The folly of this island!
They say there are but five upon this isle. We are
three of them. If the other two be brained like us,
the state totters.

STEPHANO   Drink, servant monster, when I bid you.
Your eyes are almost set in your head.

TRINCULO   Where should they be set else? He were a
brave monster indeed if they were set in his tail.

STEPHANO   My man-monster has drowned his tongue
in sack. For my part, the sea cannot drown me. I
swam, ere I could recover the shore, five and thirty

leagues off and on. By this light, you shall be my
lieutenant, monster, or my bearer.

TRINCULO Your lieutenant, if you like; he's no
bearer.

STEPHANO We'll not run, Monsieur Monster.

TRINCULO Nor walk either; but you'll lie like dogs,
and yet say nothing either.

STEPHANO Mooncalf, speak once in your life, if you
are a good mooncalf.

CALIBAN

How does your honour? Let me lick your shoe.
I'll not serve him: he is not valiant.

TRINCULO You lie, most ignorant monster! I am a
body to jostle a constable. Why, you debauched
fish, you, was there ever a man a coward that has
drunk so much sack as I today? Will you tell a
monstrous lie, being but half a fish and half a
monster?

CALIBAN Lo, how he mocks me! Will you let him,
my lord?

TRINCULO 'Lord' says he? That a monster should be
such a natural!

CALIBAN Lo, lo, again! Bite him to death, I beg.

STEPHANO Trinculo, keep a good tongue in your head.
If you prove a mutineer—the next tree! The poor
monster's my subject, and he shall not suffer
indignity.

CALIBAN I thank my noble lord. Will you be pleased
to hearken once again to the suit I made to you?

STEPHANO Sure, will I. Kneel, and repeat it. I will
stand, and so shall Trinculo.

Enter ARIEL, *invisible*

CALIBAN As I told you before, I am subject to a tyrant,
a sorcerer, that by his cunning has cheated me of
the island.

ARIEL You lie.

CALIBAN *(to Trinculo)*
 You lie, you jesting monkey, you.
 I would my valiant master would destroy you!
 I do not lie.
STEPHANO Trinculo, if you trouble him any more in
 his tale, by this hand, I will supplant some of your
 teeth.
TRINCULO Why, I said nothing.
STEPHANO Mum, then, and no more. Proceed!
CALIBAN
 I say, by sorcery he got this isle;
 From me he got it. If your greatness will
 Revenge it on him—for I know you dare,
 But this one thing dares not—
STEPHANO That's most certain.
CALIBAN
 You shall be lord of it, and I'll serve you.
STEPHANO How now shall this be compassed? Can
 you bring me to the party?
CALIBAN
 Yes, yes, my lord, I'll yield him you asleep,
 Where you may knock a nail into his head.
ARIEL You lie, you can not.
CALIBAN
 What a pied ninny is this! You scurvy fool!
 I do beseech your greatness give him blows,
 And take his bottle from him. When that's gone,
 He shall drink naught but brine, for I'll not show
   him
 Where the quick freshets are.
STEPHANO Trinculo, run into no further danger.
 Interrupt the monster one word further and, by this
 hand, I'll turn my mercy out of doors, and make a
 stockfish of you.
TRINCULO Why, what did I? I did nothing. I'll go
 farther off.

STEPHANO Did you not say he lied?
ARIEL You lie.
STEPHANO Do I so? Take you that!

He strikes TRINCULO

As you like this, give me the lie another time.
TRINCULO I did not give the lie. Out of your wits,
  and hearing too? A pox on your bottle! This can
  sack and drinking do. A murrain on your monster,
  and the devil take your fingers!
CALIBAN Ha, ha, ha!
STEPHANO Now forward with your tale.—Pray, stand
  further off.
CALIBAN

  Beat him enough. After a little time,
  I'll beat him too.
STEPHANO Stand farther.—Come, proceed.
CALIBAN

  Why, as I told you, 'tis a custom with him
  In the afternoon to sleep. There you may brain him,
  Having first seized his books; or with a log
  Batter his skull, or paunch him with a stake,
  Or cut his windpipe with your knife. Remember
  First to possess his books, for without them
  He's but a sot, as I am, and has not
  One spirit to command. They all do hate him
  As rootedly as I. Burn but his books.
  He has brave utensils, for so he calls them,
  Which, when he has a house, he will deck with.
  And that most deeply to consider is
  The beauty of his daughter. He himself
  Calls her a nonpareil. I never saw a woman
  But only Sycorax my dam and her;
  But she as far surpasses Sycorax
  As greatest does least.

STEPHANO   Is it so brave a lass?

CALIBAN
    Ay, lord. She will become your bed, I warrant,
    And bring you forth brave brood.

STEPHANO   Monster, I will kill this man. His
    daughter and I will be King and Queen—save our
    graces!—and Trinculo and yourself shall be
    viceroys. Do you like the plot, Trinculo?

TRINCULO   Excellent.

STEPHANO   Give me your hand. I am sorry I beat you;
    but while you live, keep a good tongue in your head.

CALIBAN
    Within this half hour will he be asleep.
    Will you destroy him then?

STEPHANO   Ay, on my honour.

ARIEL   This will I tell my master.

CALIBAN
    You make me merry. I am full of pleasure.
    Let us be jocund! Will you troll the catch
    You taught me but while-ere?

STEPHANO   At your request, monster, I will do
    reason, any reason. Come on, Trinculo, let us sing.

                        Sings

            Flout 'em and scout 'em,
            And scout 'em and flout 'em!
            Thought is free.

CALIBAN   That's not the tune.

ARIEL *plays the tune on a drum and pipe.*

STEPHANO   What is this same?

TRINCULO   This is the tune of our catch, played by
    the picture of Nobody.

STEPHANO   If you are a man, show yourself in your
   likeness. If you are a devil, take it as you like.
TRINCULO   O, forgive me my sins!
STEPHANO   He that dies pays all debts. I defy you.
   Mercy upon us!
CALIBAN   Are you afraid?
STEPHANO   No, monster, not I.
CALIBAN
   Be not afraid; the isle is full of noises,
   Sounds, and sweet airs, that give delight and hurt
      not.
   Sometimes a thousand twangling instruments
   Will hum about my ears; and sometimes voices
   That, if I then had waked after long sleep,
   Will make me sleep again. And then, in dreaming,
   The clouds I thought would open, and show riches
   Ready to drop upon me, that when I waked
   I cried to dream again.
STEPHANO   This will prove a brave kingdom to me,
   where I shall have my music for nothing.
CALIBAN   When Prospero is destroyed.
STEPHANO   That shall be by and by. I remember the
   story.
TRINCULO   The sound is going away. Let's follow it,
   and after do our work.
STEPHANO   Lead, monster; we'll follow. I would I
   could see this drummer. He lays it on.
TRINCULO   Will you come?—I'll follow, Stephano.

                                               Exeunt

                     SCENE III
               Another part of the island.

Enter ALONSO, SEBASTIAN, ANTONIO, GONZALO, ADRIAN,
        FRANCISCO, *and others*

GONZALO

  By our lady, I can go no further, sir.
  My old bones ache. Here's a maze trod indeed,
  Through forthrights and meanders! By your patience,
  I needs must rest me.

ALONSO

  Old lord, I cannot blame you,
  Who am myself attacked with weariness
  To the dulling of my spirits. Sit down and rest.
  Even here I will put off my hope, and keep it
  No longer for my flatterer. He is drowned
  Whom thus we stray to find, and the sea mocks
  Our frustrate search on land. Well, let him go.

ANTONIO *(aside to Sebastian)*

  I am right glad that he's so out of hope.
  Do not, for one repulse, forgo the purpose
  That you resolve to effect.

SEBASTIAN *(aside to Antonio)*

                        The next advantage
  Will we take thoroughly.

ANTONIO   Let it be tonight;

  For, now they are oppressed with travel, they
  Will not, and cannot, use such vigilance
  As when they are fresh.

SEBASTIAN *(aside to Antonio)*

                     I say tonight. No more.

Solemn and strange music; and PROSPERO *on the
top, invisible. Enter several strange shapes,
bringing in a banquet; and dance about it with
gentle actions of salutations; and, inviting the
King, etc., to eat, they depart*

ALONSO

  What harmony is this? My good friends, hark!

GONZALO   Marvellous sweet music!

ALONSO

   Give us kind keepers, heavens! What were these?

SEBASTIAN

   A living drollery. Now I will believe

   That there are unicorns; that in Arabia

   There is one tree, the phoenix' throne, one phoenix

   At this hour reigning there.

ANTONIO   I'll believe both;

   And what does else want credit, come to me

   And I'll be sworn 'tis true. Travellers never did lie,

   Though fools at home condemn them.

GONZALO   If in Naples

   I should report this now, would they believe me?

   If I should say I saw such islanders?—

   For certain, these are people of the island—

   Who, though they are of monstrous shape, yet

     note,

   Their manners are more gentle, kind, than of

   Our human generation you shall find

   Many, nay, almost any.

PROSPERO (aside)   Honest lord,

   You have said well, for some of you there present

   Are worse than devils.

ALONSO   I cannot too much muse

   Such shapes, such gesture, and such sound,

     expressing,

   Although they want the use of tongue, a kind

   Of excellent dumb discourse.

PROSPERO (aside)   Praise in departing.

FRANCISCO

   They vanished strangely.

SEBASTIAN   No matter, since

   They have left their viands behind, for we have

     stomachs.

   Will it please you taste of what is here?

ALONSO   Not I.
GONZALO

Faith, sir, you need not fear. When we were boys,
Who would believe that there were mountaineers
Dewlapped like bulls, whose throats had hanging at
    them
Wallets of flesh? Or that there were such men
Whose heads stood in their breasts? Which now we
    find
Each putter-out of five for one will bring us
Good warrant of.

ALONSO   I will stand to and feed,

Although my last—no matter, since I feel
The best is past. Brother, my lord the Duke,
Stand to, and do as we.

Thunder and lightning. Enter ARIEL, *like a harpy,*
claps his wings upon the table, and, with a quaint
device, the banquet vanishes.

ARIEL

You are three men of sin, whom destiny—
That has to instrument this lower world
And what is in it—the never-surfeited sea
Has caused to belch up you, and on this island
Where man does not inhabit, you among men
Being most unfit to live. I have made you mad;
And even with suchlike valour men hang and drown
Their proper selves.

ALONSO, SEBASTIAN, *and the others draw their swords*

                            You fools! I and my fellows
Are ministers of Fate. The elements,
Of whom your swords are tempered, may as well

Wound the loud winds, or with bemocked-at stabs
Kill the ever closing waters, as diminish
One feather in my plume. My fellow ministers
Are like invulnerable. If you could hurt,
Your swords are now too massy for your strengths,
And will not be uplifted. But remember—
For that's my business to you—that you three
From Milan did supplant good Prospero,
Exposed unto the sea, which has requit it,
Him and his innocent child. For which foul deed
The powers, delaying, not forgetting, have
Incensed the seas and shores, yea, all the creatures
Against your peace. You of your son, Alonso,
They have bereft; and do pronounce by me
Lingering perdition—worse than any death
Can be at once—shall step by step attend
You and your ways. Whose wraths to guard you
      from,
Which here, in this most desolate isle, else falls
Upon your heads, is nothing but heart's sorrow,
And a clear life ensuing.

He vanishes in thunder. Then, to soft music,
enter the shapes again, and dance with mocks
and mows, carrying out the table.

PROSPERO
Bravely the figure of this harpy have you
Performed, my Ariel: a grace it had, devouring.
Of my instruction have you nothing abated
In what you had to say. So, with good life
And observation strange, my meaner ministers
Their several kinds have done. My high charms
      work,
And these, my enemies, are all knit up

In their distractions. They now are in my power;
And in these fits I leave them while I visit
Young Ferdinand, whom they suppose is drowned,
And his and my loved darling.   *Exit*

GONZALO
In the name of something holy, sir, why stand you
In this strange stare?

ALONSO
O, it is monstrous, monstrous!
I thought the billows spoke, and told me of it;
The winds did sing it to me; and the thunder,
That deep and dreadful organ-pipe, pronounced
The name of Prospero: it did bass my trespass.
Therefore my son in the ooze is bedded, and
I'll seek him deeper than ever plummet sounded,
And with him there lie mudded.   *Exit*

SEBASTIAN   But one fiend at a time,
I'll fight their legions over.

ANTONIO   I'll be your second.
                    Exeunt Antonio and Sebastian

GONZALO
All three of them are desperate. Their great guilt,
Like poison given to work a great time after,
Now begins to bite the spirits. I do beseech you,
That are of suppler joints, follow them swiftly,
And hinder them from what this craziness
May now provoke them to.

ADRIAN   Follow, I pray you.
                                        Exeunt

Act IV

SCENE I
Before PROSPERO'S cell.

Enter PROSPERO, FERDINAND, *and* MIRANDA

PROSPERO
    If I have too austerely punished you,
    Your compensation makes amends, for I
    Have given you here a third of my own life,
    Or that for which I live; who once again
    I tender to your hand. All your vexations
    Were but my trials of your love, and you
    Have strangely stood the test. Here, before heaven,
    I ratify this my rich gift. O Ferdinand,
    Do not smile at me that I boast hereof,
    For you shall find she will outstrip all praise,
    And make it halt behind her.
FERDINAND   I do believe it
    Against an oracle.
PROSPERO
    Then, as my gift, and your own acquisition
    Worthily purchased, take my daughter; but
    If you do break her virgin-knot before
    All sanctimonious ceremonies may
    With full and holy rite be ministered,
    No sweet aspersion shall the heavens let fall
    To make this contract grow. But barren hate,
    Sour-eyed disdain and discord shall bestrew
    The union of your bed with weeds so loathly

That you shall hate it both. Therefore take heed,
As Hymen's lamps shall light you.

FERDINAND   As I hope
For quiet days, fair issue, and long life,
With such love as it is now, the murkiest den,
The most opportune place, the strongest suggestion
Our worser genius can, shall never melt
My honour into lust, to take away
The edge of that day's celebration
When I shall think that Phoebus' steeds are
    foundered
Or Night kept chained below.

PROSPERO   Fairly spoken.
Sit then and talk with her: she is your own.
What, Ariel! My industrious servant, Ariel!

Enter ARIEL

ARIEL
What would my potent master? Here I am.

PROSPERO
You and your meaner fellows your last service
Did worthily perform, and I must use you
In such another trick. Go bring the rabble,
Over whom I give you power, to this place.
Incite them to quick motion, for I must
Bestow upon the eyes of this young couple
Some vanity of my art. It is my promise,
And they expect it from me.

ARIEL   Immediately?

PROSPERO
Ay, with a twink.

ARIEL
Before you can say, 'Come' and 'Go',
And breathe twice, and cry, 'So, So',

Each one, tripping on his toe,
Will be here with mop and mow.
Do you love me, master? No?

PROSPERO

Dearly, my delicate Ariel. Do not approach
Till you do hear me call.

ARIEL   Well, I conceive.   *Exit*

PROSPERO

Look you be true. Do not give dalliance
Too much the rein. The strongest oaths are straw
To the fire in the blood. Be more abstemious,
Or else, good night your vow.

FERDINAND   I warrant you, sir,
The white cold virgin snow upon my heart
Abates the ardour of my liver.

PROSPERO   Well.
Now come, my Ariel! Bring a corollary,
Rather than want a spirit. Appear, and pertly.
No tongue! All eyes! Be silent.

Soft music. Enter IRIS

IRIS

Ceres, most bounteous lady, your rich leas
Of wheat, rye, barley, vetches, oats, and pease;
Your turfy mountains, where live nibbling sheep,
And flat meads thatched with forage them to
    keep;
Your banks with undercut and frillèd brims,
Which spongy April at behest betrims,
To make cold nymphs chaste crowns; and your
    broom-groves,
Whose shadow the dismissèd bachelor loves,
Being lass-lorn: your poll-clipt vineyard,
And your sea-marge, sterile and rocky-hard,

Where you yourself do air—the queen of the sky,
Whose watery arch and messenger am I,
Bids you leave these, and with her sovereign grace,
Here on this grass-plot, in this very place,
To come and sport. Her peacocks fly amain.

JUNO *descends*

Approach, rich Ceres, her to entertain.

Enter CERES

CERES
Hail, many-coloured messenger, that ne'er
Do disobey the wife of Jupiter;
Who, with your saffron wings, upon my flowers
Diffuse the honey-drops, refreshing showers;
And with each end of your blue bow do crown
My bosky acres and my unshrubbed down,
Rich scarf to my proud earth. Why has your queen
Summoned me hither to this short-grassed green?
IRIS
A contract of true love to celebrate,
And some donation freely to estate
On the blest lovers.
CERES   Tell me, heavenly bow,
If Venus or her son, as you do know,
Does now attend the queen? Since they did plot
The means that husky Dis my daughter got,
Her and her blind boy's scandalled company
I have forsworn.
IRIS   Of her society
Be not afraid. I met her deity

Cutting the clouds towards Paphos, and her son
Dove-drawn with her. Here thought they to have
   done
Some wanton charm upon this man and maid,
Whose vows are, that no bed-right shall be paid
Till Hymen's torch be lighted: but in vain.
Mars's hot minion is returned again;
Her waspish-headed son has broken his arrows,
Swears he will shoot no more, but play with
   sparrows,
And be a boy right out.

CERES   Highest queen of state,
Great Juno comes; I know her by her gait.

JUNO
How does my bounteous sister? Go with me
To bless this twain, that they may prosperous be,
And honoured in their issue.

They sing

JUNO
   Honour, riches, marriage-blessing,
   Long continuance, and increasing,
   Hourly joys be still upon you!
   Juno sings her blessings on you.

CERES
   Earth's increase, harvest plenty,
   Barns and garners never empty,
   Vines with clustering bunches growing,
   Plants with goodly burden bowing;
   Spring come to you at the farthest
   In the very end of harvest.
   Scarcity and want shall shun you,
   Ceres' blessing so is on you.

FERDINAND
    This is a most majestic vision, and
    Harmonious charmingly. May I be bold
    To think these spirits?
PROSPERO   Spirits, which by my art
    I have from their confines called to enact
    My present fancies.
FERDINAND   Let me live here ever!
    So rare a wondered father and a wise
    Makes this place Paradise.

Juno and Ceres whisper, and send Iris on employment.

PROSPERO   Sweet, now, silence!
    Juno and Ceres whisper seriously.
    There's something else to do. Hush and be mute,
    Or else our spell is marred.
IRIS
    You nymphs, called Naiads, of the winding brooks,
    With your sedged crowns and ever-harmless looks,
    Leave your crisp channels, and on this green land
    Answer your summons; Juno does command.
    Come temperate nymphs, and help to celebrate
    A contract of true love. Be not too late.

Enter certain Nymphs

    You sunburned sicklemen, of August weary,
    Come hither from the furrow, and be merry.
    Make holiday; your rye-straw hats put on,
    And these fresh nymphs encounter every one
    In country footing.

*Enter Reapers, properly habited. They join with
the Nymphs in a graceful dance, towards the end
whereof, Prospero starts suddenly and speaks; after*

which, to a strange, hollow, and confused noise,
they heavily vanish.

PROSPERO *(aside)*
  I had forgotten that foul conspiracy
  Of the beast Caliban and his confederates
  Against my life. The minute of their plot
  Is almost come.—Well done! Avoid! No more!—
FERDINAND
  This is strange. Your father's in some passion
  That works him strongly.
MIRANDA   Never till this day
  Saw I him touched with anger so distempered.
PROSPERO
  You do look, my son, in a movèd sort,
  As if you were dismayed. Be cheerful, sir.
  Our revels now are ended. These our actors,
  As I foretold you, were all spirits, and
  Are melted into air, into thin air;
  And, like the baseless fabric of this vision,
  The cloud-capped towers, the gorgeous palaces,
  The solemn temples, the great globe itself,
  Yea, all that it inherits, shall dissolve,
  And, like this insubstantial pageant faded,
  Leave not a rack behind. We are such stuff
  As dreams are made on; and our little life
  Is rounded with a sleep. Sir, I am vext.
  Bear with my weakness; my old brain is troubled.
  Be not disturbed with my infirmity.
  If you be pleased, retire into my cell
  And there repose. A turn or two I'll walk,
  To still my beating mind.
FERDINAND *and* MIRANDA   We wish your peace.
                              Exeunt Ferdinand and Miranda

PROSPERO
  Come with a thought. I thank you, Ariel. Come!

Enter ARIEL

ARIEL
  Your thoughts I cleave to. What's your pleasure?
PROSPERO   Spirit,
  We must prepare to meet with Caliban.
ARIEL
  Ay, my commander. When I presented Ceres,
  I thought to have told you of it, but I feared
  Lest I might anger you.
PROSPERO
  Say again, where did you leave these varlets?
ARIEL
  I told you, sir, they were red-hot with drinking.
  So full of valour that they smote the air
  For breathing in their faces, beat the ground
  For kissing of their feet; yet always bending
  Towards their project. Then I beat my drum,
  At which, like unbacked colts, they pricked their
    ears,
  Advanced their eyelids, lifted up their noses
  As they smelt music. So I charmed their ears
  That calf-like they my lowing followed, through
  Toothed briars, sharp furzes, pricking gorse, and
    thorns,
  Which entered their frail shins. At last I left them
  In the filthy mantled pool beyond your cell,
  There dancing up to the chins, that the foul lake
  O'erstunk their feet.
PROSPERO   This was well done, my bird!
  Your shape invisible retain you still.
  The trumpery in my house, go bring it hither,
  Decoy to catch these thieves.
ARIEL   I go, I go!
                               Exit

PROSPERO

A devil, a born devil, on whose nature
Nurture can never stick; on whom my pains,
Humanely taken, all, all lost, quite lost.
And as with age his body uglier grows,
So his mind cankers. I will plague them all
Even to roaring.

Enter ARIEL, *loaded with glistering apparel, etc.*

Come, hang them on this line.

Enter CALIBAN, STEPHANO, *and* TRINCULO, *all wet*

CALIBAN

Pray you, tread softly, that the blind mole may not
Hear a foot fall. We now are near his cell.

STEPHANO   Monster, your fairy, which you say is a
harmless fairy, has done little better than played
the Jack with us.

TRINCULO   Monster, I do smell all horse-piss, at which
my nose is in great indignation.

STEPHANO   So is mine. Do you hear, monster? If I
should take a displeasure against you, look you—

TRINCULO   You were but a lost monster.

CALIBAN

Good my lord, give me your favour still.
Be patient, for the prize I'll bring you to
Shall hoodwink this mischance. Therefore, speak
    softly.
All is hushed as midnight yet.

TRINCULO   Ay, but to lose our bottles in the pool—

STEPHANO   There is not only disgrace and dishonour
in that, monster, but an infinite loss.

TRINCULO   That's more to me than my wetting. Yet
this is your harmless fairy, monster.

STEPHANO   I will fetch off my bottle, though I am
  over ears for my labour.

CALIBAN
  Pray you, my king, be quiet. See you here,
  This is the mouth of the cell. No noise, and enter.
  Do that good mischief which may make this island
  Your own for ever, and I, your Caliban,
  For aye your foot-licker.

STEPHANO   Give me your hand. I do begin to have
  bloody thoughts.

TRINCULO   O King Stephano! O peer! O worthy
  Stephano, look what a wardrobe here is for you!

CALIBAN
  Let it alone, you fool! It is but trash.

TRINCULO   O ho, monster! We know what belongs to
  a frippery. O King Stephano!

STEPHANO   Put off that gown, Trinculo. By this hand,
  I'll have that gown!

TRINCULO   Your grace shall have it.

CALIBAN
  The dropsy drown this fool! What do you mean
  To dote thus on such luggage? Let it alone,
  And do the murder first. If he awakes,
  From toe to crown he'll fill our skins with pinches,
  Make us strange stuff.

STEPHANO   Be you quiet, monster. Mistress line, is
  not this my jerkin? Now is the jerkin under the
  line. Now, jerkin, you are like to lose your hair and
  prove a bald jerkin.

TRINCULO   Do, do! We steal by line and level, if it
  likes your grace.

STEPHANO   I thank you for that jest. Here's a garment
  for it. Wit shall not go unrewarded while I am king
  of this country. 'Steal by line and level' is an
  excellent pass of wit. There's another garment for
  it.

TRINCULO   Monster, come put some lime upon your
  fingers, and away with the rest.

CALIBAN
  I will have none of it. We shall lose our time,
  And all be turned to barnacles, or to apes
  With foreheads villainous low.

STEPHANO   Monster, lay to your fingers. Help to bear
  this away where my hogshead of wine is, or I'll
  turn you out of my kingdom. Go to, carry this!

TRINCULO   And this.

STEPHANO   Ay, and this.

  A noise of hunters heard. Enter divers Spirits *in
  shape of dogs and hounds, hunting them about,*
  PROSPERO *and* ARIEL *setting them on.*

PROSPERO   Hey, Mountain, hey!

ARIEL   Silver! There it goes, Silver!

PROSPERO   Fury, Fury! There, Tyrant, there! Hark,
  hark!

  CALIBAN, STEPHANO, *and* TRINCULO *are driven out.*

  Go, charge my goblins that they grind their joints
  With dry convulsions, shorten up their sinews
  With agèd cramps, and more pinch-spotted make
    them
  Than leopard or mountain-cat.

ARIEL   Hark, they roar!

PROSPERO
  Let them be hunted soundly. At this hour
  Lie at my mercy all my enemies.
  Shortly shall all my labours end, and you
  Shall have the air at freedom. For a little
  Follow, and do me service.   *Exeunt*

Act V

SCENE I
Before PROSPERO'S cell.

Enter PROSPERO, *in his magic robes, and* ARIEL

PROSPERO
Now does my project gather to a head.
My charms crack not, my spirits obey, and time
Goes upright with its carriage. How's the day?
ARIEL
On the sixth hour, at which time, my lord,
You said our work should cease.
PROSPERO   I did say so,
When first I raised the tempest. Say, my spirit,
How fare the King and his followers?
ARIEL   Confined together
In the same fashion as you gave in charge,
Just as you left them—all prisoners, sir,
In the line-grove which weather-fends your cell.
They cannot budge till your release. The King,
His brother, and yours, abide all three distracted,
And the remainder mourning over them,
Brimful of sorrow and dismay. But chiefly,
Him that you termed, sir, the good old lord
    Gonzalo,
His tears run down his beard like winter's drops
From eaves of reeds. Your charm so strongly works
    them
That if you now beheld them your affections
Would become tender.
PROSPERO   Do you think so, spirit?

ARIEL

Mine would, sir, were I human.

PROSPERO   And mine shall.

Have you, which are but air, a touch, a feeling
Of their afflictions, and shall not myself,
One of their kind, that relish all as sharply,
Passion as they, be kindlier moved than you are?
Though with their high wrongs I am struck to the
    quick,
Yet with my nobler reason against my fury
Do I take part. The rarer action is
In virtue than in vengeance. They being penitent,
The sole drift of my purpose does extend
Not a frown further. Go release them, Ariel.
My charms I'll break, their senses I'll restore,
And they shall be themselves.

ARIEL   I'll fetch them, sir.

Exit

PROSPERO

You elves of hills, brooks, standing lakes, and
    groves,
And you that on the sands with printless foot
Do chase the ebbing Neptune, and do fly him
When he comes back; you demi-puppets that
By moonshine do the green, sour ringlets make,
Whereof the ewe not bites; and you whose pastime
Is to make midnight mushrooms, that rejoice
To hear the solemn curfew, by whose aid—
Weak masters though you are—I have bedimmed
The noontide sun, called forth the mutinous winds,
Between the green sea and the azured vault
Set roaring war; to the dread rattling thunder
Have I given fire, and rifted Jove's stout oak
With his own bolt; the strong-based promontory
Have I made shake, and by the spurs plucked up
The pine and cedar; graves at my command

Have wakened their sleepers, opened, let them forth
By my so potent art. But this rough magic
I here abjure, and when I have required
Some heavenly music—which even now I do—
To work my end upon their senses that
This airy charm is for, I'll break my staff,
Bury it certain fathoms in the earth,
And deeper than did ever plummet sound
I'll drown my book.

Solemn music
Here enters ARIEL *before; then* ALONSO *with a*
frantic gesture, attended by GONZALO: SEBASTIAN
and ANTONIO *in like manner, attended by*
ADRIAN *and* FRANCISCO. *They all enter the circle*
which PROSPERO *had made, and there stand*
charmed; which PROSPERO *observing, speaks.*

A solemn air, and the best comforter
To an unsettled fancy, cure your brains,
Now useless, boiled within your skull. There stand,
For you are spell-stopped.
Holy Gonzalo, honourable man,
My eyes, even sociable to the show of yours,
Let fall fellowly drops. The charm dissolves apace,
And as the morning steals upon the night,
Melting the darkness, so their rising senses
Begin to chase the ignorant fumes that mantle
Their clearer reason. O good Gonzalo,
My true preserver, and a loyal sir
To him you follow, I will pay your graces
Home both in word and deed. Most cruelly
Did you, Alonso, use me and my daughter.
Your brother was a furtherer in the act.
You are pinched for it now, Sebastian. Flesh and
    blood,

You, brother mine, that entertained ambition,
Expelled remorse and nature, who, with
    Sebastian—
Whose inward pinches therefore are most strong—
Would here have killed your king, I do forgive you,
Unnatural though you are. Their understanding
Begins to swell, and the approaching tide
Will shortly fill the reasonable shore
That now lies foul and muddy. Not one of them
That yet looks on me, or would know me. Ariel,
Fetch me the hat and rapier in my cell.
I will unclothe me, and myself present
As I was sometime Milan. Quickly, spirit!
You shall ere long be free.

ARIEL sings and helps to attire him.

ARIEL

    Where the bee sucks, there suck I,
    In a cowslip's bell I lie;
    There I couch when owls do cry.
    On the bat's back I do fly
    After summer merrily.
    Merrily, merrily shall I live now,
    Under the blossom that hangs on the bough.

PROSPERO

Why, that's my dainty Ariel! I shall miss you,
But yet you shall have freedom—so, so, so.
To the King's ship, invisible as you are!
There shall you find the mariners asleep
Under the hatches. The Master and the Boatswain
Being awake, enforce them to this place,
Immediately, I pray.

ARIEL

I drink the air before me, and return
Ere ever your pulse twice beats.   *Exit*

GONZALO
    All torment, trouble, wonder, and amazement
    Inhabit here. Some heavenly power guide us
    Out of this fearful country!
PROSPERO   Behold, sir King,
    The wronged Duke of Milan, Prospero.
    For more assurance that a living prince
    Does now speak to you, I embrace your body,
    And to you and your company I bid
    A hearty welcome.
ALONSO   Whether you are he or no,
    Or some enchanted trifle to abuse me,
    As late I have been, I not know. Your pulse
    Beats as of flesh and blood; and, since I saw you,
    The affliction of my mind amends, with which
    I fear a madness held me. This must crave—
    If this should be at all—a most strange story.
    Your dukedom I resign, and do entreat
    You pardon me my wrongs. But how should
      Prospero
    Be living, and be here?
PROSPERO   First, noble friend,
    Let me embrace your age, whose honour cannot
    Be measured or confined.
GONZALO   Whether this is
    Or is not, I'll not swear.
PROSPERO   You do yet taste
    Some subtleties of the isle, that will not let you
    Believe things certain. Welcome, my friends all!
    (*aside to* SEBASTIAN *and* ANTONIO)
    But you, my brace of lords, were I so minded,
    I here could pluck his highness' frown upon you,
    And justify you traitors. At this time
    I will tell no tales.
SEBASTIAN   (*aside*) The devil speaks in him.

PROSPERO   No.
  For you, most wicked sir, whom to call brother
  Would even infect my mouth, I do forgive
  Your rankest fault—all of them; and require
  My dukedom of you, which perforce, I know,
  You must restore.

ALONSO   If you are Prospero,
  Give us particulars of your preservation;
  How you have met us here, whom three hours since
  Were wrecked upon this shore; where I have lost—
  How sharp the point of this remembrance is!—
  My dear son Ferdinand.

PROSPERO   I am sad for it, sir.

ALONSO
  Irreparable is the loss, and patiènce
  Says it is past her cure.

PROSPERO   I rather think
  You have not sought her help, of whose soft grace
  For the like loss, I have her sovereign aid,
  And rest myself content.

ALONSO   You the like loss?

PROSPERO
  As great to me, as late, and supportable
  To make the dear loss, have I means much weaker
  Than you may call to comfort you, for I
  Have lost my daughter.

ALONSO   A daughter?
  O heavens, that they were living both in Naples,
  The King and Queen there! That they were, I wish
  Myself were mudded in that oozy bed
  Where my son lies. When did you lose your
    daughter?

PROSPERO
  In this last tempest. I perceive these lords
  At this encounter do so much wonder

That they devour their reason, and scarce think
Their eyes do offices of truth, their words
Are natural breath. But, howsoever you have
Been jostled from your senses, know for certain
That I am Prospero, and that very Duke
Who was thrust forth of Milan, who most strangely
Upon this shore, where you were wrecked, was
   landed
To be the lord of it. No more yet of this,
For it is a chronicle of day by day,
Not a relation for a breakfast, nor
Befitting this first meeting. Welcome, sir.
This cell's my court. Here have I few attendants,
And subjects none abroad. Pray you, look in.
My dukedom since you have given me again,
I will requite you with as good a thing,
At least bring forth a wonder to content you,
As much as me my dukedom.

Here PROSPERO *discovers* FERDINAND *and* MIRANDA,
playing at chess.

MIRANDA
  Sweet lord, you play me false.
FERDINAND   No, my dearest love,
  I would not for the world.
MIRANDA
  Yes, for a score of kingdoms you should wrangle,
  And I would call it fair play.
ALONSO   If this proves
  A vision of the island, one dear son
  Shall I twice lose.
SEBASTIAN   A most high miracle.
FERDINAND
  Though the seas threaten, they are merciful.
  I have cursed them without cause.

He comes forward, and kneels.

ALONSO   Now all the blessings
  Of a glad father compass you about!
  Arise, and say how you came here.
MIRANDA   O, wonder!
  How many goodly creatures are there here!
  How beauteous mankind is! O brave new world,
  That has such people in it!
PROSPERO   It is new to you.
ALONSO
  What is this maid with whom you were at play?
  Your eldest acquaintance cannot be three hours.
  Is she the goddess that has severed us,
  And brought us thus together?
FERDINAND   Sir, she is mortal;
  But by immortal Providence, she's mine.
  I chose her when I could not ask my father
  For his advice, nor thought I had one. She
  Is daughter to this famous Duke of Milan,
  Of whom so often I have heard renown,
  But never saw before; of whom I have
  Received a second life; and second father
  This lady makes him to me.
ALONSO   I am hers.
  But, O,.how oddly will it sound that I
  Must ask my child forgiveness!
PROSPERO   There, sir, stop.
  Let us not burden our remembrances with
  A heaviness that's gone.
GONZALO   I have inly wept,
  Or should have spoken ere this. Look down, you
    gods,
  And on this couple drop a blessèd crown!
  For it is you that have chalked forth the way
  Which brought us hither.

ALONSO   I say amen, Gonzalo.

GONZALO

  Was Milan thrust from Milan that his issue
  Should become kings of Naples? O, rejoice
  Beyond a common joy, and set it down
  With gold on lasting pillars. In one voyage
  Did Claribel her husband find at Tunis,
  And Ferdinand her brother found a wife
  Where he himself was lost; Prospero his dukedom
  In a poor isle, and all of us ourselves
  When no man was his own.

ALONSO *(to Ferdinand and Miranda)*

                       Give me your hands.
  Let grief and sorrow still embrace his heart
  That does not wish you joy.

GONZALO   Be it so! Amen.

    Enter ARIEL, *with the* Master *and* Boatswain
        amazedly following.

  O look sir, look sir, here is more of us!
  I prophesied, if a gallows were on land,
  This fellow could not drown. Now, blasphemy,
  That swear grace overboard, not an oath on shore?
  Have you no mouth by land? What is the news?

BOATSWAIN

  The best news is that we have safely found
  Our King and company; the next, our ship—
  Which, but three glasses since, we gave out split—
  Is tight and ready, bravely rigged, as when
  We first put out to sea.

ARIEL *(aside to Prospero)* Sir, all this service
  Have I done since I went.

PROSPERO *(aside to Ariel)* My tricksy spirit!

ALONSO
      These are not natural events. They strengthen
      From strange to stranger. Say, how came you hither?
BOATSWAIN
      If I did think, sir, I were well awake,
      I'd strive to tell you. We were dead of sleep
      And—how we know not—all clapped under hatches;
      Where, but even now, with strange and several
            noises
      Of roaring, shrieking, howling, jingling chains,
      And more diversity of sounds, all horrible,
      We were awaked; straightway at liberty.
      Where we, in all our trim, freshly beheld
      Our royal, good, and gallant ship, our Master
      Capering to eye her. On a trice, so please you,
      Even in a dream, were we divided from them,
      And were brought moping hither.
ARIEL   *(aside to Prospero)*   Was it well done?
PROSPERO   *(aside to Ariel)*
      Bravely, my diligence. You shall be free.
ALONSO
      This is as strange a maze as ever men trod,
      And there is in this business more than nature
      Was ever conduct of. Some oracle
      Must rectify our knowledge.
PROSPERO   Sir, my lord,
      Do not infest your mind with beating on
      The strangeness of this business. At picked leisure—
      Which shall be shortly—single I'll resolve you,
      Which to you shall seem probable, of every
      These happened accidents. Till when, be cheerful,
      And think of each thing well. *(aside to Ariel)* Come
            hither, spirit.
      Set Caliban and his companion free.

Untie the spell.   *Exit Ariel*
                How fares my gracious sir?
There are yet missing of your company
Some few odd lads that you remember not.

Enter ARIEL, *driving in* CALIBAN, STEPHANO, *and*
TRINCULO *in their stolen apparel.*

STEPHANO Every man shift for all the rest, and let no
    man take care for himself, for all is but fortune.
    Coragio, bully-monster, coragio!
TRINCULO If these are true spies which I wear in my
    head, here's a goodly sight!
CALIBAN
    O Setebos, these are brave spirits indeed!
    How fine my master is! I am afraid
    He will chastise me.
SEBASTIAN   Ha, ha!
    What things are these, my lord Antonio?
    Will money buy them?
ANTONIO   Very like. One of them
    Is a plain fish, and no doubt marketable.
PROSPERO
    Mark but the badges of these men, my lords,
    Then say if they are true. This misshapen knave,
    His mother was a witch, and one so strong
    That could control the moon, make flows and ebbs,
    And deal in her command without her power.
    These three have robbed me, and this demi-devil—
    For he's a bastard one—had plotted with them
    To take my life. Two of these fellows you
    Must know and own. This thing of darkness I
    Acknowledge mine.
CALIBAN   I shall be pinched to death.
ALONSO
    Is not this Stephano, my drunken butler?

SEBASTIAN

He is drunk now. Where had he wine?

ALONSO

And Trinculo is reeling ripe. Where should they
Find this grand liquor that has gilded them?
How came you in this pickle?

TRINCULO   I have been in such a pickle since I saw
you last that I fear me will never out of my bones.
I shall not fear fly-blowing.

SEBASTIAN   Why, how now, Stephano?

STEPHANO   O, touch me not! I am not Stephano, but
a cramp!

PROSPERO   You would be king of the isle, fellow?

STEPHANO   I should have been a sore one, then.

ALONSO

This is a strange thing as ever I looked on.

PROSPERO

He is as disproportioned in his manners
As in his shape.—Go, fellow, to my cell.
Take with you your companions. As you look
To have my pardon, trim it handsomely.

CALIBAN

Ay, that I will; and I'll be wise hereafter,
And seek for grace. What a thrice double ass
Was I to take this drunkard for a god,
And worship this dull fool!

PROSPERO   Go to. Away!

ALONSO

Hence, and bestow your luggage where you found it.

SEBASTIAN

Or stole it, rather.

                    Exeunt Caliban, Stephano, and Trinculo

PROSPERO

Sir, I invite your highness and your train
To my poor cell, where you shall take your rest
For this one night; which, part of it, I'll waste

With such discourse as, I not doubt, shall make it
Go quick away—the story of my life,
And the particular accidents gone by
Since I came to this isle. And in the morn,
I'll bring you to your ship, and so to Naples,
Where I have hope to see the nuptials
Of these our dear-belovèd solemnized;
And thence retire me to my Milan, where
Every third thought shall be my grave.

ALONSO   I long
To hear the story of your life, which must
Take the ear strangely.

PROSPERO   I'll deliver all,
And promise you calm seas, auspicious gales,
And sail so expeditious, that shall catch
Your royal fleet far off.—My Ariel, chick,
That is your charge. Then to the elements
Be free, and fare you well.—Please you, draw near.

                                                    Exeunt

EPILOGUE

Spoken by PROSPERO

Now my charms are all o'erthrown,
And what strength I have's my own,
Which is most faint. Now 'tis true
I must be here confined by you,
Or sent to Naples. Let me not,
Since I have my dukedom got
And pardoned the deceiver, dwell
In this bare island by your spell;
But release me from my bands
With the help of your good hands.

Gentle breath of yours my sails
Must fill, or else my project fails,
Which was to please. Now I want
Spirits to enforce, art to enchant;
And my ending is despair,
Unless I be relieved by prayer,
Which pierces so, that it assaults
Mercy itself, and frees all faults.
As you from crimes would pardoned be,
Let your indulgence set me free.   *Exit*